M000086372

THE *MIRACLE* of CONVERSION

Pacific Press® Publishing Association
Nampa, Idaho
Oshawa, Ontario, Canada
www.pacificpress.com

Cover design by Steve Lanto
Cover design resources from John Steel
Inside design by Aaron Troia

Except where otherwise noted, all Scripture quotations in this book are from the King James Version.

Scripture quotations marked NIV are from the HOLY BIBLE, NEW INTERNATIONAL VERSION®. Copyright © 1973, 1978, 1984 by International Bible Society. Used by permission of Zondervan Publishing House. All rights reserved.

Scripture texts credited to NRSV are from the New Revised Standard Version of the Bible, copyright © 1989 by the Division of Christian Education of the National Council of the Churches of Christ in the USA. Used by permission. All rights reserved.

Scripture texts credited to ASV are from the American Standard Version. Copyright © 1901. Public Domain.

Scriptures quoted from RSV are from the Revised Standard Version of the Bible, copyright © 1946, 1952, 1971 by the Division of Christian Education of the National Council of the Churches of Christ in the U.S.A. Used by permission.

You can obtain additional copies of this book by calling toll-free 1-800-765-6955 or by visiting http://www.adventistbookcenter.com.

Library of Congress Cataloging-in-Publication Data:

The miracle of conversion / [compiled by] Morris Venden.
   p. cm.
 ISBN 13: 978-0-8163-2342-5 (pbk.)
 ISBN 10: 0-8163-2342-9 (pbk.)
 1. Conversion—Christianity. I. Venden, Morris L.
 BV4921.3.M57 2009
 248.2'4—dc22

                                                           2009003554

09 10 11 12 13 • 5 4 3 2 1

DEDICATION

To my wife, Marilyn,

and my three children, Lee, Lynn, and LuAnn,

for their remarkable loyalty and support

for me and my work.

ALSO BY MORRIS VENDEN

CONTENTS

PREFACE

This book is about conversion—the most neglected topic in the Christian church. To the careful searcher, it is also the most important topic. Ellen White called it the greatest miracle.[1]

Recently, I checked with our Seventh-day Adventist publishing houses to see how many books they have published on conversion. The answer was zero! I checked in the Southern Baptist Seminary library in Fort Worth, Texas, and discovered only five books on conversion. Four of them are of extremely limited valuue. The first chapter in this book comes from the fifth book, the only good one.

Then I went to the CD-ROM disk of Ellen G. White's writings. There I found nine thousand references on this topic. Wow! I concluded from what I found there that the conversion of our children should be the most important concern of parents and teachers and that presenting our doctrines to anyone is pointless until we know that person has been converted.

Conversion is essential to our understanding of God's will and to our following Christ. This book is an anthology of the best material I have found on this important topic.

---

1. Ellen G. White, *Evangelism* (Washington, D.C.: Review and Herald®, 1946), 290.

Chapter 1

THE NECESSITY OF
CONVERSION

E. STANLEY JONES

This chapter is taken from a book that E. Stanley Jones wrote, titled Conversion. *Jones spent his life leading people in India to be converted. His book on conversion is the only one I have found on this topic that I consider to be of value. It shows the necessity of conversion—that it isn't optional for the Christian life. Enjoy!*

We divide humanity into many classes—white and black, rich and poor, educated and uneducated, Americans and non-Americans, East and West. Modern Japanese youth divide people into "wet" and "dry"—the "wet" are those who observe customs and morality, and the "dry" are those who do as they like! But Jesus drew a line down through all these distinctions and divided humanity into just two classes—the unconverted and the converted, the once-born and the twice-born. All men live on one side or the other of that line. No other division matters—this is a division that divides; it is a division that runs through time and eternity. "Verily, verily, I say unto thee, Except a man be born again, he cannot see the kingdom of God" (John 3:3). "Except ye be converted, and become as little children, ye shall not enter into the kingdom of heaven" (Matthew 18:3).

What did Jesus mean by being "born again" and being "converted"? Obviously, He meant something very, very important, for having it or not having it divides men—all men—for time and eternity. Part of the answer lies in the difference between proselytism and conversion. Many people consider them to be the same thing, but nothing could be further from the thought of Jesus than to make them one—He rejected one and insisted on the other. He said to the religious leaders of that day: "Ye compass sea and land to make one proselyte, and when he is made, ye make him twofold more the child of hell than yourselves" (Matthew 23:15). He rejected this scramble for numbers that only added to their collective egotism—an essentially irreligious process. Proselytism is a change from one group to another that doesn't necessarily involve any change in character and life. It is a change of label but not of life. Conversion, on the other hand, is a change in character and life, followed by an outer change of allegiance corresponding to that inner change. A Hindu said to me one day, "I'll become baptized if you give me twenty thousand rupees and a good job." I replied, "My brother, if you should lay down twenty thousand rupees at my feet and say, 'Please baptize me,' I would refuse it—and you!" Proselytism and conversion are poles apart, and to confuse them is to degrade the most precious thing that life holds— conversion. It is to confuse love and lust, beauty and ugliness, life and death.

Moreover, to confuse being converted with being inside the church and being unconverted with being outside the church is to fall into the same fatal error, for Jesus urged this necessity of being born again upon Nicodemus, a highly respectable religious "teacher of Israel." Why did He say straight off, "You must be born again" (see John 3:7)? The reason obviously was that He saw Nicodemus steal in at night, looking this way and that way before he entered, afraid of what people would say about his coming to see this young Disturber of the *status quo*. Some people are self-centered, some herd-centered, and some are God-centered. Nicodemus belonged to a combination of the first two, not to the last. So Jesus had gently put him on the side of those who do not see the kingdom of God.

But was this an arbitrary division imposed on life—imposed by a gentle fanatic—or did Jesus not impose something on life but expose something out of life? Does life too say, "You must be born again," and "Except you be converted, you cannot enter the kingdom of God"? Is life rendering the same verdict that Jesus pronounced two thousand years ago and with increasing insistence and urgency? Listen to what is revealed in doctors' offices where the disrupted are passing on the illness of their minds and souls to their bodies; to what the patients on psychiatrists' couches are saying as they reveal their mental and emotional and spiritual tangles; to what lies back of a façade of respectability in homes where marital conflicts cause people to teeter on the verge of breakdown and breakup; to what management and labor are saying as their strained relations harden into sullen hostility or open conflict; to what parents and children say as unconverted parents are irritated to distraction at seeing their children practicing their own sins; to what self-centered and egotistical national representatives are unconsciously saying as they stumble from failure to failure to find agreements—agreements that affect the destiny of us all; to what many a heart filled with the sheer boredom and emptiness of life is saying silently; to what the conscience is saying as it is gnawed at night and day by a sense of estrangement through guilt. Listen to life as it *is* and you will hear in an increasing crescendo, "You must be born again. Except you be converted, you cannot live now or hereafter." The whole of life is a commentary on what I've just said.

A ROLL CALL OF WITNESSES

Do we need to call the roll of witnesses to the fact that life breaks down without conversion? Here is what H. G. Wells wrote shortly before his death: "A frightful queerness has come into life. Hitherto events have been held together by a certain logical consistency as the heavenly bodies have been held together by the golden cord of gravitation. Now it is as if that cord had vanished and everything is driven anyhow, anywhere, at a steadily increasing velocity. The writer is convinced that there is no way out or around, or through the impasse. It is the end."

Here was a great mind, without an inner sustaining conversion, up against a blank wall of futility—"It is the end." But through conversion, that end could become a beginning, as it has for many—for as many as have tried it.

Said one of the greatest statesmen of our time to me, "I'm fed up." His patriotism and his devotion, without conversion, had run their course and were not sufficient to sustain him. Another great statesman said just recently to me, "We've reached bottom." Life without conversion had no sustaining hope. Another in high office said, "My religion and my philosophy have let me down. So I hate my work, and I hate life." His "religion" and his "philosophy" didn't provide for conversion, so they let him down.

A Japanese governor introduced me in these words: "I'm a man here tonight without a faith. I wish I had a faith. I envy those of you who do have a faith. But I'm a lost sheep. I've come here tonight to gain a faith if possible through the speaker. And I hope you will gain one too." And he was a trustee of a Buddhist temple.

A Japanese doctor told me that tuberculosis had been ousted as killer number one in Japan in favor of heart disease and high blood pressure. When I asked him the cause, he replied, "Spiritual uneasiness." At the close of the war,* the philosophy of a great people had collapsed—they were not a divine people with a divine emperor who had a divine destiny to rule. That conception of life went down in blood and ruin and left a vacuum. So this sense of vacuum has sent up the blood pressure of a whole nation.

Carl Jung, the great psychiatrist, said, "The central neurosis of our time is emptiness." Human nature simply can't stand emptiness and meaninglessness. It gets jumpy, jittery, and goes to pieces.

The tragic thing is that this sense of meaninglessness has become a characteristic of our modern culture. Professor W. T. Stace of Princeton University said, "It is the essence of the modern mind that the universe is meaningless and purposeless." The modern mind has given us knowledge and conveniences—and emptiness!

---

*World War II.

An undergraduate of one of our great universities told Sam Shoemaker: "I don't know what is the matter with me, but I feel lost." Dr. Shoemaker quoted that remark to a number of his contemporaries and about nine out of ten replied, "That's me."

That sense of lostness has produced a sense of cynicism and a lack of faith in anything or any person. A young man asked a professor of history, "What's your racket?" The professor replied that he was a professor of history and then asked, "Aren't you interested in history?" "Naw," the young man replied. "I'm willing to let bygones be bygones." He wasn't interested in anything, for nothing gave a basic meaning and goal to life. He needed conversion.

Leigh Hunt, speaking of Napoleon's final weeks when he escaped from Elba and made his stand at Waterloo, wrote, "No great principle stood by him." That is at the bottom of the sense of lostness in the soul of modern man. No great principle stands by them. They feel orphaned, estranged, alone—terribly alone. An atheist has been defined as "a man who has no invisible means of support." But many who wouldn't want to be called atheists have that same sense of lacking invisible support. They go down under the pressure of circumstances, for they have no invisible means of support.

I saw a man stagger through a railway station in Japan with a huge carton on his bent back. On the carton were the words, "The Universe." An individual bent under the weight of the universe! That graphically describes what has happened to the individual. Through books, newspapers, radio, and television, the "universe" and its troubles are daily laid on the backs of staggering individuals. In addition, they have to bear their own individual burdens within their heart. When people have no sustaining conversion, it's no wonder that so many crack up under their burdens.

SUFFERING FROM NOTHINGNESS

In India, a man spoke to a Rotary Club for an hour on "nothing." This nothingness, *sunyavadi,* has been built up into a philosophy.

Having nothing to sustain them, people capitalize it and take refuge in nothingness. So the empty take refuge in emptiness, but you cannot change emptiness into fullness by capitalizing it. Emptiness has to be changed into fullness by conversion. An Indian Christian said of a certain man, "He is suffering from nothingness." Many do.

A pastor's brilliant son, a personnel man in a great corporation, told his father, "I'm trying hard to be an atheist, but I'm having a time of it!" He and his nurse wife are each spending forty dollars a week with the same psychiatrist. Conversion would take their feet off the flypaper of self-preoccupation and send them on their way, rejoicing because they would be released.

A sister told of her brother, who does not go to church, that he had said, "I don't need the money, but I work just to run away from myself." His wife added, "I work to keep from committing suicide." Conversion would put back meaning and value and goals into life. They muddle through without it.

Sir Titus Salt, inventor of alpaca and founder of Saltaire, heard a preacher say he saw a caterpillar crawl up a painted stick in search of a juicy twig only to have to retrace his steps. There are the painted sticks of pleasure, wealth, power, and fame. Men climb them only to have to retrace their steps. The next day, the baronet visited the preacher and said, "I have been climbing those painted sticks. I'm a weary man. Is there rest for a weary millionaire?" He found rest and release through the words of Jesus, "Come unto me, all ye that labour and are heavy laden, and I will give you rest" (Matthew 11:28). Conversion turned weariness into worthwhileness.

A Hindu atheist said to me, "I'm like a broken radio receiving set trying to get the wavelength." An inquirer came in just after I had my talk with the atheist, and I called him back and asked if he wouldn't interpret for me as I talked to this inquirer in a language I didn't know. He gladly assented. An atheist interpreting the Christian message to an inquirer! He did it enthusiastically, adding emphasis to my points. For the first time in his life, he came in contact with something positive, something hopeful, something constructive. He was only a transmitter, but the feel of it was good. The finding of it would be what he was really wanting amid all his atheism.

What shall we say of those who take refuge in narcotics? It's an escape out of futility. I talked to an alcoholic. I felt he was agreeing with me about everything, so I suggested that we get down on our knees, thinking he would gladly lay his troubled life at the feet of Christ. But he stiffened, sat bolt upright, and said between clenched teeth, "I'll be darned if I do." So I prayed without him. When I was interrupted by a noise, I opened my eyes and saw that he had slipped away into the bathroom to get a swig of liquor to sustain him through the ordeal of resisting salvation. He had always turned to liquor as the way out, and in the greatest crisis of his life, he turned to it again. He wanted a refuge from salvation! Later, on his deathbed, he turned feebly to God, surrendering his ruined life to save his ruined soul. And the love that had followed him all those years embraced him and bade heaven rejoice. Conversion would have saved his life as well as his soul.

In a city were two signs side by side: "Go to church. Find strength for your life," and "Where there's life, there's Budweiser." These two signs represent two approaches to life—one is from the inward to the outward; the other is the outward to the inward. One depends on inward salvation from guilt and fear and conflict; the other depends on outward stimulants— pick-me-ups that let you down. The increase in narcotic consumption and tranquilizers is the outer symptom of a deep need for conversion. It is the pagan substitute for conversion—with pathetic results.

When we turn to the philosophers and psychiatrists and writers and novelists, we hear the same sense of inadequacy, often deepening into despair. Dr. William E. Hocking, Harvard philosopher, said at the Jerusalem Conference that man brings himself up to a certain place and then finds he hasn't the resources to complete himself. He must be completed from without, by something beyond himself. I held my breath waiting to see whether he would say the word, but he didn't. At the close I said, "Dr. Hocking, why didn't you say the word?"

"What word?" he asked.

I replied, "When you said man hasn't enough resources to complete himself, but must be completed by something outside himself, why didn't you say, 'Conversion, new birth, born from above'?"

He thoughtfully replied, "I'm a philosopher, I can't say the word. You are a missionary and an evangelist; you can say the word."

"But," I replied, "I'm not willing for you to turn it over to me. If you see it, you should say it."

Whether through implication or by revealing silences, philosophy does say the word—it points to the need of conversion, of being born from above.

PHILOSOPHERS OF DESPAIR

Listen to this despairing word from an Eastern philosopher: "A blind turtle and an ox yoke are floating on a vast ocean, and the turtle has as much chance of putting his head through that yoke as you have of being reborn as a man and not an animal." A Western philosopher, Bertrand Russell, is of the same mood when he suggests as the remedy "an unyielding despair."

Men respond to these philosophers of despair, for they represent their own mood. "Who then speaks most powerfully to and for the men of this generation? Those poets, artists, and philosophers who preach despair and sing of bleak encounter with silence and futility and nonbeing."[1]

These writers can say, "In my nostrils there is the odor / Of Death and Dissolution," but only the Christian faith with its belief in conversion can end by saying, "But there is also the fragrance / Of an Eternal Spring."[2]

When we turn to pagan psychiatry, we find that same sense of final futility—man hasn't enough resources in himself to complete himself. In establishing a Christian psychiatric center, Nurmanzil Psychiatric Center, Lucknow, India, we defined the relationship of Christianity and psychiatry thus: "Psychiatry carried on under Christian auspices and with the Christian motive and spirit has as its aim to help the patient to become mentally and emotionally sufficiently foot-loose to make an intelligent surrender of himself to God; and to provide techniques to develop the new life." The end of the whole process is to get the patient off his own hands into the hands of God, for the basic cause of his mental and emotional upset is self-centered preoccupation.

Pagan psychiatry has no way of getting that release, for it has no purpose or method of self-surrender to God. The patient is supposed to be cured by self-knowledge—a fallacy. If the self-knowledge doesn't lead him to self-surrender to God, then it leaves him turning round on himself, which is the disease itself, however filled with knowledge it may be.

Freud, the high priest of pagan psychiatry, said, "In our view the truth of religion may be altogether disregarded. . . . Dark, unfeeling, and unloving powers determine human destiny." As for me, I would suspect a premise that brought me to the conclusion that "dark, un-feeling, and unloving powers determine human destiny"—for if I be-lieve that, then it cuts the nerve of my faith in the possibility of hu-man nature's being changed. Conversion is ruled out, and with conversion ruled out, there is nothing to do but to sink back into the fatalities of unfeeling and unloving forces residing in the subcon-scious.

A psychiatrist called up a friend of mine, a minister, and asked, "Can you help me? These patients hang on my belt as though I were God. They call me up at two, three, or four o'clock in the morning to talk with me. It's getting on my nerves. I can't stand it." The minister suggested the book *The Way*. The psychiatrist read seven pages and was converted then and there—gloriously converted. He told the pas-tor that he had been charging fifty dollars an hour for treatment, and he also added that often when patients were about to be discharged, he would raise another issue and string them out—at fifty dollars an hour! After his conversion, he cut his prices to eight dollars an hour and did a lot of free work. He became tremendously excited over this matter of Christianity. A new possibility opened up before him and his patients—conversion. The fatalism of being in the grip of dark, unfeeling, and unloving powers was broken—broken by conversion, a conversion that brought him into saving contact with the power of light and love and life.

No wonder a leading psychologist told Bryan Green, "I need a religious experience myself for my patients need it and I can't give it to them unless I have it myself." Another psychologist said, "I always send my patients to the church, for there the forgiveness of sins is preached." A psychiatrist who dealt—at high fees—with the disrupted of Hollywood said, "All these patients of mine need is a mourner's bench."

These pointed words by Dr. Henry Sloane Coffin sum up the trend:

> Current psychology adds to these moral alibis. Men and women have themselves analyzed, and find emancipation in banishing the ugly names which vigorous religion attached to sins, where these are re-christened with labels with no suggestion of guilt. They are maladjusted, or introverted, rather than dishonest or selfish. A middle-aged father tires of his wife and becomes involved with a young woman half his age, and is told by a practitioner that he is suffering from "a spasm of re-adolescence," when he ought to be struck in the face with "Thou shalt not commit adultery."[3]

When we turn to the scientists, we find ourselves smiling a wry smile at the statement of Adam Smith in the beginning days of modern science: "Science is the great antidote to the poison of enthusiasm and superstition. When we have learned to make sensible use of science the world will not be filled with war, ignorance, prejudice, superstition and fear." We smile especially at those last two words "and fear"! At this very moment, we are in the grip of a world fear brought on by the creation of atomic bombs by science. Some of the makers of the atomic bombs called together the ministers around Chicago and in a two days' conference announced, "Frankly, we're frightened. We can produce the means in atomic energy, but we can't produce the ends for which those means are to be used. Unless you ministers can produce the moral and spiritual ends for which atomic energy is to be used, then we're sunk." Science turned to religion and cried, "Save us or we perish." And they meant it, for they saw that unless a conversion—individual and collective—that would turn atomic energy from destruction to construction took place, we would be sunk, literally sunk. The need is simple and profound—conversion!

The founder of American behaviorism, Dr. John B. Watson, tells us, "We need nothing to explain human behavior but the ordinary laws of physics and chemistry." I am reminded of saying to Dr. George Carver, the great Black saint and scientist, that a professor of chemistry had said to me that life was no more than a flaring up of a flame from the combustion of chemical elements. The great chemist shook his head and said, "The poor man, the poor man!" That was all! And it was enough, for anyone who holds that human behavior and human life can be explained in terms of physics and chemistry is a poor man with a poor view of life and with a poor power to help human behavior and human life. He needs conversion in his viewpoint and in person.

INSIDE THE CHURCH TOO

Does organized religion speak of the need of conversion? It certainly does—and with louder and louder insistence. When the Archbishop's Report on Evangelism said, "The Church is more a field, rather than a force, for evangelism," it spoke the sober truth. Probably two-thirds of the membership of the churches know little or nothing about conversion as a personal, experimental fact. That should not discourage us about the church, for hospitals are out to banish disease and yet they are filled with diseased people. Only a few—the doctors and attendants—are well. Schools are out to banish ignorance and yet they are filled with ignorant students. The church is out to banish sin and yet it is filled with sinful people. That is not to be wondered at, nor need it give us concern. Instead, we must ask, are the people inside the churches being converted? Or are they, having come into the church, settling down to half conversions, living in half lights—or worse, in complete emptiness—under the respectable umbrella of the church? The acid test of the validity of a Christian church is whether it can not only convert people from the outside to membership but also produce conversion within its own membership. When it can't do both, it is on its way out.

Many within the churches have their motives and conduct determined by other than Christian sources. Carl Jung says, "His decisive motives, interests and impulses do not come from the sphere of Christianity, but from the unconscious and undeveloped soul, which is just as pagan and archaic as ever." Here Jung says that the behavior of the person described is determined by the subconscious and not from Christian sources. A British cabinet minister commented to a friend, "I can't say that being a Christian seriously affects the decisions I make, the way I make them, or my relation with others." What can you expect in the laity if the ministers, too, lack conversion? A senior in a theological seminary asked, "What do you mean by 'being born again'?" He hadn't run across it in the seminary. A student who had just passed out from the seminary asked me, "What do you mean by 'self-surrender'? I never heard the word in the seminary." The preface of a book on pastoral counseling contains these words: "Let no one think he will be converted through the reading of this book." When I laid it down, I thought to myself, *No danger of anyone being converted through the reading of that book. He never gets near it.* The word *self-surrender* was not used in the book nor hinted at. The counseling was about marginal issues with the essential self untouched, hence unconverted.

A Polish Catholic courted an American girl. While attending a Protestant church with her, he got up from her side and went to the altar. The girl said to herself, "Here I am praying for my Roman Catholic husband-to-be, and he goes forward, while I, an unconverted Methodist, don't go forward." She went forward, and they were both converted. They called up the Methodist pastor to tell him the good news. He was cold. "You'll get over that. It often happens." They couldn't get what they wanted in that church so they went to another.

A lady asked a minister, "What does the Cross mean?" The minister replied, "Well, I don't know a better way to decorate the top of a church, do you?" A down-to-earth woman summed it up in these words: "You can no more tell what you don't know than you can come back from where you ain't been." Unconverted or half-converted ministers in the pulpit produce unconverted or half-converted people in the pews. Someone facetiously defined a Methodist as "a man who has just enough religion to make him feel uneasy in a cocktail bar and not enough religion to make him feel at home in a prayer meeting." If anyone of another denomination reading the above is about to throw the first stone at the Methodists, it might be well for him to look into a mirror first! Sam Shoemaker says pointedly that "many are not converted, but a little civilized by their religion."

I picked up my bottle of Viet, my grass vitamin tablets. The wrapper of the bottle came off in my hand, leaving the bottle standing. As I stood there with the wrapper in my hand, I read the various items in the vitamin content. I could have become vitamin-starved reading the contents without taking the tablets themselves. Many take the table of contents of religion, its doctrines, its beliefs, but they don't take the thing itself—Christ the Redeemer and Savior—to convert and save them. They starve while reading the menu!

Many are so afraid of the hot pots that they forget that the bigger danger is the cold pots, who outnumber the hot pots a hundred to one. These outwardly in but not inwardly in church members need one thing and only one thing supremely—conversion. When a bishop announced a Quiet Day for the clergy, one of them wrote back and said, "What my parish needs is not a Quiet Day but an earthquake." Augustine describes such unconverted Christians as "frost-bound Christians." They need the warm glow of the Spirit's converting power to unfreeze them. One of this type prayed in a prayer meeting, "O God, if any spark of divine grace has been kindled in this meeting, water that spark." A lot of people are in the business of watering sparks! To change the figure, many belong to "the mothball fleet of Christians—immobilized Christians."

One of the finest men in the American pulpit said, "I went to the altar twice because I was preaching an insipid gospel. Here this visitor comes and preaches the gospel with such freshness and power that people hold their hats and hold on to their benches."

From the pew at Keuka Ashram, New York, someone said, "I deliberately set out to make myself a shallow person. I find it easier. But it hurts my faith, and it hurts me." Of one church member it was said, "She believed a little bit in everything and nothing in anything." In the voting in India with two hundred million potential voters, many of whom were illiterate, they got over the difficulty by placing the party ballot boxes in a row with a symbol on each box representing a party. One man tore his ballot into small bits and dropped a piece in each of the ten boxes. He voted for all—and none! Dr. Samuel Johnson once said roundly, "Sir, a man may be so much of everything that he is nothing of anything." Many people are so open-minded that their minds are like a sieve; they can't hold a conviction.

FULL OF WIGGLE-TAILS

What about those who once knew conversion but in whom it has faded out? One man said in a testimony meeting, "Twenty years ago I was converted and got my pitcher full and since then nary a drop has gone in and nary a drop has gone out." Someone remarked, "Then I'm sure by now it is full of wiggle-tails." Most people need a rebirth in their forties on general principles. Hazlitt wrote of the middle-aged Coleridge, "All that he had done of moment, he had done twenty years ago; since then he may be said to have lived on the sound of his own voice." Many are living spiritually on the sound of their own voices—echoes of the past instead of an experience of the present. Harnack, the great church historian, tracing this inner evaporation, says, "The original enthusiasm evaporates and the religion of law and form arises." Said a high churchman, "I don't care what happens to the outside world just so I can say Mass every morning." A Mass but no message!

What shall we say of the absorption in trivial church duties in lieu of this divine contagion? Of one man it was said, "He increased his pace the more he realized that he had lost the way." Busyness takes the place of blessedness. I sat in the early devotional hour on a hillside and watched a dog excitedly wagging his tail with his head in the bushes. I expected him to jump a rabbit at any moment, but he was only after crickets. All that time and energy and attention over crickets! Many of our church activities could be classed as cricket attention. We are busy at nothingnesses!

A great deal of missionary work is left undone because the missionary is absorbed in the missionary and his problems. I said to a missionary about to be sent home, "What do you think is the basis of your trouble?" She replied, "I'm sitting in a powder keg." When I asked, "What is the powder keg?" she replied, "Myself. I'm two persons—one a person who didn't want to come to the mission field and the other, one who was afraid I'd be lost if I didn't." I said, "You can't afford to be either one of these persons, can you, for they are both unsatisfactory. You need to decide to be a new person, different from each—to be converted." She assented that that was the only way out. It is the only way out—for everybody, East and West. No wonder a Danish doctor in an African mission field told me, "Ninety-nine percent of the missionaries who are sent home from the mission field go on account of emotionally and mentally induced illnesses." A change of climate wouldn't make them well—a surrender to God would.

Alexander Pope, the writer, muttered, "O Lord, make me a better man," and his spiritually enlightened page replied, "It would be easier to make you a new man." People need not to be patched up, but to be made over, to be converted, to be born again. A businessman said to a group, "I want to be born." His experience of life had led him to that conclusion. The fact is that all life is taking us by the hand and is leading us to the necessity of conversion.

Someone asked George Whitefield why he preached so often on the text, "Except a man be born again he cannot see the kingdom of God." He replied, looking the questioner in the face, "Because you must be born again." Whitefield had preached on that text over three hundred times. Life itself is preaching on that text from doctors' offices, from psychiatrists' couches, from conference rooms, from factories, from international conferences, from our homes, and, if we know ourselves, from our hearts. Someone in our ashram said, "Brother Stanley would be a mess without the Holy Spirit." And she was right—profoundly right. We are all messes without the Holy Spirit—without Him in converting, regenerating power. Our homes are messes too. Someone has said, "Ninety percent of homes have a problem unsolved."

A brilliant pagan told a minister friend of mine, "You don't need to create any demand for your wares. The demand is chemical; it exists already in everybody." The demand for conversion is not merely written in the texts of Scripture—it is written into the texture of our beings and in the texture of our relationships. Life just can't live unless it is converted to a higher level. It goes from tangle to tangle and from mess to mess and from problem to problem. All life echoes the words of Sir Philip Sidney, "O make in me these civil wars to cease," for every man who is not at peace with God has a civil war within himself. If you won't live with God, you can't live with yourself. The psychologist William James tells us, "The hell to be endured hereafter of which theology tells, is no worse than the hell we make for ourselves in this world by habitually fashioning our characters in the wrong way."

All of these things we have mentioned in this chapter—and more—converge on one thing, the necessity of conversion for the good, the bad, and the indifferent. Without it, the good are not good enough, the bad are too bad to be changed, and the indifferent can't be awakened. What Jesus preached and offered, life is echoing—with increased emphasis: "Ye must be born again."

This chapter comes from the book by E. Stanley Jones, Conversion *(Nashville: Abingdon, 1959). Used by permission. Like all the following chapters, it has been edited lightly for consistency and clarity.*

1. Julian N. Hartt, *Toward a Theology of Evangelism* (Nashville: Abingdon, 1955), 15.
2. Ibid., 24.
3. Henry Sloane Coffin, *Joy in Believing* (New York: Charles Scribner's Sons, 1956), 96.

Chapter 2

BORN TWICE?

LEE VENDEN

We now consider what conversion is all about and how it takes place. Conversion, or the new birth, happens when we come to the end of our own resources and come to Jesus in complete dependence on Him instead of ourselves. It is a supernatural work of the Holy Spirit upon the human heart that produces a change of attitude toward God and creates a capacity for knowing Him that we didn't have before. When we are born again, instead of opposing God, we are on His side, and we have a relish for spiritual things that were foolishness to us while we were at enmity to God.

I grew up being friends with Kelly. Our parents attended school together, and as the years passed, our families often enjoyed each other's company. My friendship with Kelly continued through elementary school, high school, and college. We did a lot together and enjoyed talking about all kinds of things. We gave each other encouragement and advice, and I remember romances that were improved because I followed Kelly's counsel.

On more than one occasion, friends of mine suggested that I consider dating Kelly. And many of Kelly's friends suggested that she and I would make a great couple. At first neither of us gave the matter much serious thought. Then our parents began dropping hints in that direction, and I remember taking a new look at Kelly.

She was cute, bright, fun to be around, athletic, outdoorsy, and spiritual—all qualities I deemed necessary for a life companion. I'm not sure how many of those adjectives Kelly felt applied to me, but we both decided to seriously pursue a romance together.

Then came an insurmountable problem. Neither of us seemed able to fall in love with the other. We tried! We went on official dates. We worked at it. We agreed that we were *right* for each other. We couldn't imagine having more in common with anyone else. We discussed our inability to "click." But try as we might, there was no red-hot flame. In fact, there wasn't even a spark. It was really quite discouraging to have finally found that *perfect person* and then realize that you would rather swallow gravel than kiss, snuggle, or hold hands. We finally gave up trying.

A few years later, I met Marji. The chemistry was there from the start. We didn't try to make it happen, it just did. It was more than a spark too—it was a nuclear reaction, and less than a year later, we were married. We have been kissing, snuggling, and holding hands ever since. The difference between those relationships was a "click" that transformed the second one into love.

Breathless cadavers and self-willed romances have something in common with a message Jesus gave to Nicodemus. They were talking one night about conversion—a "second birth" that Jesus said was necessary before anyone could see the heavenly kingdom. Nicodemus asked Jesus, "How can a person be born again?" *That's a good question.*

The subject of conversion is critical, but is it also problematic because you can't convert yourself. Conversion is a miracle. So if someone tells you that you need to be converted and you're not converted, what can you do about it? Can you raise the dead? Can you make yourself fall in love with Jesus by an act of your will? Can you simply say, "I'm going to fall in love with Jesus—I'm going to appreciate Him and be filled with warm thoughts and earnest devotion"? Is there *anything* you can do? Did Jesus give any clues to Nicodemus?

Before we look at what Jesus told Nicodemus, however, let's first look at Nicodemus himself. What kind of guy was he?

For starters, you're not a member of the Sanhedrin if you're not highly educated. Nicodemus was a "can do" guy. He was what we might call a fourth-generation church member.

The first time Jesus cleansed the temple, Nicodemus had been standing behind a pillar, watching. He saw what happened after the merchants had been sent out—the crowds came in for healing and comfort. Since that time, he had been searching the Scriptures, trying to find out more about the predicted work of the Messiah. He had begun to feel convicted that Jesus was special and that there was some link between Him and the prophecies that he was reading in the Old Testament.

He inquired to find out where Jesus stayed at night, and finally, under the cover of darkness, he met Jesus. He began by offering a compliment: "Rabbi, we know You're a Teacher come from God." He was trying to pave the way for a religious discussion. "Could we talk about religion?"

It is possible for me to fool myself into thinking I'm a Christian because I can talk for a long time about a scriptural theme. I'm not saying that religious studies aren't important, but just studying religious material doesn't make me a Christian.

So Nicodemus, this highly educated religious leader who believes that Jesus is special, asks to have a discussion. Jesus looks within him and says something that must have startled Nicodemus. He says, "I'm going to tell you the truth—unless a man is born again, he cannot see the kingdom of heaven" (see John 3:3).

For years, I assumed that what Jesus meant was "unless you have a conversion experience, you can't go to heaven." Careful reading indicates something different from that interpretation. Nicodemus asks if they can talk about spiritual things, and Jesus instantly replies, "Nicodemus, until you have a rebirth or conversion experience, you can't even *see* spiritual things. They don't even register in your mind. We can't talk about them, because you aren't going to grasp them. You don't have a clue. Spiritual things are spiritually discerned, and spiritual discernment happens only to people who have converted hearts."

CAN YOU SEE THIS?

Inside Seattle's Pacific Science Center is a display that tests for color blindness. It consists of thirty individual squares of multicolored shapes and patterns—each with a number camouflaged in its center. People with normal vision can easily see each number. However, a color-blind person can't see some of the numbers no matter how hard they try.

As I looked at the display, I realized that I couldn't see a number in square 11. The interpretative material said that if I didn't see a number in that square, I was color-blind to red. I've always assumed that I can see red, so I asked my daughter if she saw a number in square 11. "Sure," she said. "I see a thirteen."

A few minutes later, my son came along. I called him over. "What do you see in this square?" I asked, pointing.

"I see a thirteen," he said.

I asked him to show me where in the square it was, so he walked over and traced a 13 with his finger. "It's right here, Dad," he said. But even as he traced, I saw no number.

Suddenly, I recalled numerous times when my family and I had been traveling in the mountains and I had failed to see flowers they saw beside the road. When I looked in the direction they pointed, I would see the lupines and Shasta daisies, but I seldom saw the Indian paintbrush they claimed were there too. Not unless I got out of the car and looked closer could I see those red flowers. I realized then that I can see red but not when it's embedded in or surrounded by other colors.

For thirty-six years, I hadn't realized I had that problem. I knew *what* I should be seeing. I had *read* what to look for. People that I knew, loved, and trusted told me *they* saw it. They tried to help me see it. They testified that it was there. They traced the numbers with their fingers, but I still couldn't see them. Something would have to happen to my eyes—a miracle of restoration would have to take place in order for me to see that color.

That describes exactly the problem we have with unconverted hearts. It's not our fault that we can't see a 13 in square 11. So don't beat yourself up if you can't see. Like the blind men who asked Jesus to open their eyes (Matthew 20:30–34), you were born unable to see. Seeing is a miracle from heaven.

So Jesus says, "Nick, you can't even *see* the kingdom of heaven until you're born again." Nick had come to talk theology, to talk about religious things, but Jesus was telling him something we all need to understand. Jesus was saying, "It is not theoretical knowledge you need as much as spiritual regeneration. You don't need to have your curiosity satisfied; you need to have a new heart. You must receive new life from above before you can appreciate heavenly things. Until this change takes place, and makes all things new, our discussing My story or mission will result in no saving good."

Did you catch how important conversion is? Don't forget whom Jesus is talking to! A highly educated, denominationally employed, fourth-generation church member. Nicodemus had heard John the Baptist preach, but he'd felt no conviction. He was a "good liver"—he wouldn't think of doing anything wrong. He had a high moral standard. He was benevolent. He was noted for his generosity. He paid a faithful tithe and was liberal in supporting the church with his dollars as well as his energy. He felt secure, and he was startled that there could be a kingdom too pure for him to enter or see.

Nicodemus was struggling. He didn't want to think that he could be missing something. He was doing all he knew in order to have it right. To be told that something was missing just didn't feel good.

Jesus had said, "Unless a man be born again, he can't even see the kingdom of heaven." So Nicodemus asks the question that I hope you ask, " 'How can a man be born when he is old?' " (John 3:4, NIV). How can it happen? He couldn't seem to understand. *We* can't understand. *We* can't see the number in the square.

In answer to Nicodemus's question, Jesus says, "I'm going to tell you the truth. Unless a man is born of water, and of the Spirit, he cannot enter the kingdom of heaven" (see verse 5).

What's Jesus saying now? He's saying, "Nicodemus, you want to be born again? Well, I'll tell you something. *You* don't have any control over that. It's a Spirit thing. It's supernatural."

Jesus didn't theologize; He didn't debate, but *He did talk about the Spirit.* "Nicodemus, you know how the wind blows? Look, the trees are rustling right now. When the wind blows, you can't see the wind, but you can see the effects of the wind. That's the way it is with the Spirit. You can't see the Spirit, but when He does His work on your heart, you will then be able to see the effect. You will *understand.* There will be a difference. It will be *your* experience, but the *Spirit* will be the One causing it. You could say that it's the Spirit that gives birth" (see verses 6–8).

Is it all clear to you now? Would *you* be feeling better if you'd been Nicodemus? I can almost hear him saying, "Well, OK then! That takes care of everything. Thank You for all these fine answers! I came here to talk about spiritual things, and You tell me I can't see them unless I'm born again. I ask how that can happen, and You tell me it's something supernatural that I have no control over.

"Let's get practical! If I can't *make* it happen, is there anything I *can do* that would place me in a more likely or receptive position for the Spirit to do whatever it is You say *He* has to do? There must be something I can do" (see verse 9).

REMEMBER THE SNAKE?

Here comes Jesus' benchmark statement on the subject of conversion. Here is His answer to Nicodemus's question about whether there is anything *we* can do to avail ourselves of the Spirit's work. In John 3:14, 15, Jesus refers Nicodemus to a story found in Numbers 21:7–9 about a bronze serpent that effected a cure.

Do you recall reading about those people dying from snakebites?

Moses was instructed to put a serpent on a pole, remember? What happened after that? If you read it again, you'll discover that anybody who looked in the direction of the uplifted serpent was healed—immediately, miraculously, supernaturally.

Suppose you were bitten by a rattlesnake and you went to a hospital and the emergency room doctor opened up an encyclopedia to a page containing a picture of a rattlesnake and said, "Here, if you will just look at this picture for a few minutes, you'll be fine." I bet you'd say, "What kind of doctor is this? I'm dying of snakebite, and he tells me to look at a snake?"

What was happening in Israel's encounter with those snakes? Something supernatural! It didn't matter if you had been playing with snakes when you got bit—if you looked, you lived. It didn't matter if you had been bitten once before and were healed, then got bitten again and came back to the bronze serpent. No, if you looked again, you were healed again—regardless of how many times you'd been bitten. It didn't matter whether you deliberately chose to be bitten or if your being bitten was simply an accident; if you looked at the bronze snake, you were *healed.* There was life in a look. It happened miraculously. It was supernatural. And the miracle happened only to people who looked. If you didn't look, you died.

Nicodemus asks if there's anything he *can do,* and Jesus says, "Yes! Look in the direction of the uplifted Savior. Focus your eyes on Him, and the Spirit will do whatever else needs to happen. You want to do something? Look My way. 'I, when I am lifted up from the earth, will draw all people to myself' " (John 12:32, NRSV).

The soul is not enlightened by proof texts, discussion, debate, or argument. We must look at Jesus to live. Nicodemus received this lesson and began searching the Scriptures in a new way—not for the discussion of a theory but in order to receive life for his soul.

Jesus is saying, "If you look My direction, the Spirit will work in your heart and you will experience the new birth." You don't have to wait for a preacher to lift Jesus up. You can do that yourself, on a daily basis.

John the Baptist said, "Behold the lamb of God" (John 1:29). Pilate said, "Behold the man!" (John 19:5). I wonder if either of them realized they were summarizing the how-to of the gospel in a sentence. *Look!* There's life in a look. Look at the uplifted Savior. Look at the crucified Savior. Look at Jesus.

I'd like to suggest that you read the Gospel of John. Don't focus on how many people were fed, or how many miracles there were, or which miracle preceded which miracle. Don't read for *information*—read for your soul. Before you begin reading, say a prayer something like this: "Lord Jesus, what I really want is a new heart. What I really want this morning is a new birth, and I can't make it happen. I can't soften and subdue my heart, but I understand that if I look Your way, the Spirit will do something for me that I can't do for myself. So I'm going to look, and I'm asking You to make it worthwhile. I'm asking You to make the miracle take place. I'm asking You to enable me to see the number thirteen in square eleven. Please make Yourself real for me today."

Pray that prayer and look His way, and don't just do it once or twice. Keep looking day after day after day—every morning. If Paul is right in saying that we die daily (1 Corinthians 15:31), then the new birth, conversion, has to be a daily experience as well.

No one ever comes to Jesus who doesn't first feel a need for something better. Nobody.

There are two ways to feel a need for Jesus. The best way to gain a sense of need is to look at Him. Lift Him up by reading about Him, meditating on Him, and talking to Him in prayer. As you bow at the foot of the cross and look at Jesus, you will see yourself as sinful and needy, but you will also see Him as *Savior*. That is the shortest route.

But there's another way. It's the way the majority of us do it, and it's the long route home. George McDonald, an author whom C. S. Lewis credits with being instrumental in his conversion, describes it this way: God loves you and longs for companionship with you. He loves you so much that He will try to woo you to Himself with blessings untold, gift upon gift, favor upon favor. If you fail to respond to His wooing, He loves you so much that He will send out the big dogs of heaven to nip your heels and chase you His direction.

You can wait for the big dogs. You can wait for trouble, failure, heartache, disappointment, and brokenness. You can wait until your world has collapsed and you're lying flat on your back with nowhere to look but up. Or you can choose, as Nicodemus did, to look *now* at the uplifted Savior with the purpose of becoming better acquainted with Him as your Friend. "Look unto me," He says, "and be ye saved" (Isaiah 45:22).

FOR ME, IT HAPPENED LIKE THIS

As a senior in high school, I was a fourth-generation Christian who knew the answers, knew the doctrines, knew my church's fundamental beliefs, had attended church schools all my life but didn't know Jesus for myself. I was a preacher's kid who pretty much stayed out of trouble, but other than church, I had no personal, private time for God. I knew *about* the truth, but I didn't know the One who *is* the Truth. In fact, I didn't even realize that I could or should know Jesus as a personal Friend.

One Friday evening, I stopped by a friend's house, looking for something to do. He invited me to join him and another friend in attending a small Bible study group. These friends were the sort who enjoyed experimenting with drugs for nonmedicinal reasons, and I was incredulous. I said, "*You and Randy* are going to a Bible study group?"

"Yeah," he said a little hesitantly, "both of us."

A group of about twelve kids from our high school had decided that they wanted to find God. They'd gone to one of our teachers and said, "A group of us would like to get to know Jesus, and we wondered if you'd let us come to your house on Friday nights to read about Him." He said he would be delighted to share his home for such an activity. So every Friday night, he turned his living room over to this group and with his family retreated to the back rooms of the house.

The group had been meeting for some time with a very simple agenda. They read about the life of Christ in the Gospels, they talked with each other about what Jesus meant to them and what they meant to Jesus, and they prayed. That's all they did. Just those three things. And now I was being invited to attend.

"Isn't there something better we could do on Friday night?" I asked.

"Why don't you just give it a try?" Chris said.

I was unaware that during their study, this group had stumbled onto the concept of intercessory prayer—praying for others. They had begun an experiment by praying for one guy and one girl from school who seemed seriously uninterested in spiritual things. They wanted to find out if praying for others had any effect, and they had chosen some hard cases so they'd be sure to know if it worked. I don't remember who the girl was, but I do know the name of the guy. They prayed for me without even asking if I minded.

That Friday night, I reluctantly decided to go. But I determined that I would go as the devil's advocate. My plan was to raise some unanswerable religious questions and then watch them bend their brains out of shape trying to give answers. I had one in particular—regarding free choice and God's foreknowledge—that I was certain would send them for a loop.

Imagine my surprise when I discovered that this group hadn't come to discuss religion. (Remember Nicodemus?) They were there to talk about Jesus: what He meant to them and what they were discovering that *they* meant to Him. It's very, very difficult to talk about "religious stuff" when everyone wants to focus on Jesus. I ended up sitting there speechless as these kids shared from their hearts what Jesus was doing in their lives and why they loved Him.

When people tell you what Jesus means to them, you can't argue with them. You can't get into a debate the way you can when discussing doctrine and proof texts. You can say you don't believe what they are saying, but they don't care, because like Paul, they "know whom [they] have believed, and [are] convinced that he is able to guard what

[they] have entrusted to him" (2 Timothy 1:12, NIV). They're beaming with the joy of knowing Jesus, and your disbelief doesn't rob them of a thing!

For an hour and a half, I watched and listened. Finally they said, "We're going to have prayer now. We're going to kneel and pray conversationally. No one really says 'Amen.' We just pray little sentences until it seems clear that we're through. And nobody prays unless they want to." Then they knelt, but I didn't. They bowed their heads and closed their eyes, but I didn't. I kept mine open to see what these people were going to do.

They began to talk to Jesus. They didn't say, "Please bless the missionaries and leaders of our country." They talked to Jesus as a person talks to their best friend. I felt as though I was eavesdropping on a bunch of private conversations. That living room seemed as though it could have been the throne room of heaven.

Without my knowing it, they were also praying inaudibly. You see, when I walked through the door to join their group that night, they were blown away. Nobody said anything to me about it, of course, but I was one of the prayer experiments, and I had *come.* They gave each other discreet signs and determined that they weren't going to quit praying for me *that night.* And so, silent prayers were ascending all evening that the Spirit would heal a snake-bitten guy as he looked in the direction of the uplifted serpent.

BREAKTHROUGH

It happened! When my closest friends started praying and talking to Jesus as you'd talk to a friend, I found myself weeping. I couldn't understand it. I hadn't come there to weep, yet suddenly, I was overcome with tears. I hung my head so they wouldn't see me crying. Prayer finally ended, and everybody left except my two friends. They came over and talked to me about what was happening. They talked about the second birth and how all things become new. They told me about Jesus wanting to be my *Friend,* and it clicked. Suddenly I understood for the first time that *Christianity is not about what you do, but about* who *you know!* And I went home a new creation.

I got home after midnight, woke up early the next morning, and read the entire book of Romans. *This is amazing,* I thought. *This stuff about faith and trust and getting to know a Friend is all right here.* I had never read the Bible through converted eyes before.

As my dad walked by my open door and saw me reading my Bible, he did a double take. Quickly turning around, he ran down the hallway and told my mother, "Lee is reading his Bible!" She couldn't believe it either and had to walk by to see for herself.

When I came out of my room, they were eating breakfast. As I sat down to join them, I could hardly contain my enthusiasm for the wonderful new light I wanted to share. Excitedly, I said, "Dad, did you know—Christianity is not about what you *do*. It's about who you *know*. In fact, Jesus is more interested in becoming our Friend than He is in our performance because He knows that if we can become friends, *that* will change us! Isn't that cool?"

I love my preacher father for his response that morning. He didn't say to me, "You idiot! That's been the only string on my violin for the past twenty years. Where was your head when you were in church?" No, he didn't say that. All he said was "Isn't that *wonderful?*"

Then I went to church and stayed for both services. Can you imagine my surprise when Dad began to preach about the very stuff I'd told him at breakfast? I couldn't believe he'd managed to work that into his sermon on such short notice!

What had happened? Had my father changed his sermon for me? No, I suddenly could see the number 13 in square 11. A miracle had happened. How had it happened? I had put myself in a place where the Son was lifted up, and the Holy Spirit drew me to Jesus.

I am glad that Jesus wants to do for us exceedingly, abundantly, above all that we could ask or think (Ephesians 3:20). I'm thankful that He has promised to do for us what we cannot do for ourselves. May He help us to recognize our great need and save us from waiting until He lets the "big dogs" loose. May His Spirit create in us new hearts, enabling us to see Jesus more clearly and love Him more dearly.

Lift Him up every day. Be born again. There is life in a look—at Jesus.

This chapter comes from the book by Lee Venden, It's All About Him *(Hagerstown, Md.: Review and Herald®, 2004). Used by permission.*

Chapter 3

THE HOLY SPIRIT AND CONVERSION

MORRIS VENDEN

First Corinthians 2:14 says, "The natural man receiveth not the things of the Spirit of God: for they are foolishness unto him, neither can he know them, because they are spiritually discerned." In order to serve God aright, we must be born of the Divine Spirit. This will purify the heart and renew the mind, giving us a new capacity for knowing and loving God. The Holy Spirit convicts the sinner, converts the sinner, cleanses the Christian, and commissions for service. In the chapter that follows, we will consider especially His work of conversion. When we understand what conversion is, we can know whether or not we have been converted.

John 16:7–11 begins with an interesting clause: " 'But I tell you the truth . . .' " (NIV).

Wait a minute—this is Jesus speaking! Didn't Jesus *always* tell the truth? Apparently He was trying to draw particular attention to what was to follow.

" 'But I tell you the truth: It is for your good that I am going away. Unless I go away, the Counselor will not come to you; but if I go, I will send him to you.' " Then Jesus goes on to describe the work of this Counselor: " 'he will convict the world of guilt in regard to sin and righteousness and judgment.' " Of sin " 'because men do not believe in me.' " Of righteousness " 'because I am going to the Father, where you can see me no longer.' " And of judgment " 'because the prince of this world now stands condemned.' "

An essential part of the Holy Spirit's work is to convict the world of its sinful condition, and our greatest need in *accepting* salvation is to realize our great need *for* salvation. In other words, our greatest need is to see our need! Otherwise, we will never be motivated to come to Jesus and accept the salvation He offers.

This passage in John 16 also assures us that the Holy Spirit will convict the whole world of sin. His work isn't confined to a particular locality or group of people. It's a world mission, a world work. The Spirit of God is given freely so that *everyone* can have the opportunity to receive "the true light that gives light to every man . . . coming into the world" (John 1:9, NIV). Thus people who refuse to accept salvation do so through their own willful refusal of the gift of life.

Even among the so-called heathen, the Spirit's power is felt. There are those who have never received light from human sources, yet worship God. They know little of theology, but they cherish God's principles. Though ignorant of God's written law, they have heard His voice speaking to them in nature and have done the things that the law requires. Their works are evidence that the Holy Spirit has touched their hearts, and they are recognized as God's children.

WHAT IS SIN?

John 16 not only tells us that Jesus says the Holy Spirit will convict of sin, but in verse 9 it gives us His definition of what sin is, " 'in regard to sin, because men do not believe in me.' " Jesus doesn't say people are convicted of sin because they kill or lie or commit adultery. He doesn't say they're convicted of sin because they break God's law. Jesus says that they're convicted of sin because of a lack of belief in Him!

Now this belief includes much more than mental assent. James 2:19 tells us that even the devils believe—and tremble. Back in the days when Jesus was here on earth, His own disciples sometimes doubted His divinity; the priests and rulers were unable to recognize Him as the Messiah; even the common people, although they gladly heard His words, often questioned among themselves whether He was a prophet. But the devils believed and freely confessed that He was the Christ, the Holy One of God (Mark 1:24).

So, the sin that the Holy Spirit convicts us of is much more than mere mental assent. It's a lack of faith that reaches down to the very depths of our hearts—a lack of *trusting*. The Holy Spirit brings the conviction that we've been living in rebellion against God, trying to control our lives with our own power regardless of how moral or immoral we've been. The Holy Spirit leads us into a faith relationship with Jesus—a relationship that results in our *trusting* Him because we really *know* Him. And because we know Him, we have learned to love Him and surrender to Him.

Unfortunately, we seldom have a true picture of our own hearts. Jeremiah 17:9 reminds us that "the heart is deceitful above all things, and desperately wicked: who can know it?" It's all too easy for us to be deceived about our own spiritual condition. It may not be hard for me to be aware of *your* sin, but *my* condition? That's another matter! We may be acutely aware of the sins of those around us and yet be totally blind when it comes to our own hearts. Only the Holy Spirit can open our eyes to that!

The Holy Spirit works to bring us to that sense of need—and then lifts up Jesus to fulfill it. There's a case history of the Holy Spirit's convicting power recorded in Acts 2. Peter gave the sermon on that Day of Pentecost. He began with a bit of history, a bit of genealogy, a bit of eschatology, and then quoted a bit of prophecy from Joel. But when he got to the heart of his message—Jesus Christ, crucified and risen from the dead—the people were "cut to the heart," and they interrupted Peter's sermon by giving their own altar call! They cried out, " 'Brothers, what shall we do?' " (verse 37, NIV). They were obviously under conviction—and it happened when Jesus was uplifted!

Now that's the right kind of altar call! No soft lights, no tear-jerking stories, no music to work on the emotions. Just a true picture of Jesus and His love for us. The Holy Spirit went to work—and three thousand were converted that day!

We can be thankful for this first mighty work of the Holy Spirit that convicts us of sin. But the Spirit doesn't stop there! It's not enough for the sword of the Spirit to pierce the heart and bring conviction, necessary as that may be. In order for us to have salvation, we must not only see our need but also understand the *solution* to our need. The Spirit doesn't wound us and then leave us bruised and bleeding. He wounds that He may heal. He cuts deep with His sword that He may pour in healing and bring about complete and total restoration. And when He has brought conviction to our hearts, His work is only just beginning.

THE SPIRIT AND CONVERSION

When we're born into this world of sin, we're born without an understanding of the joy of holiness or communion with God. Yet we *are* born with an uncontrollable desire to worship! Even secular psychologists and sociologists have discovered that human beings inevitably choose to worship *something*. There seems to be a deep need, a vacuum in the human heart, that demands an object for worship. But until we discover the truth of the gospel—that this vacuum is God-shaped—we're never truly satisfied. We continue to worship things or other people or even ourselves, but fulfillment and happiness always remain just around the corner.

We aren't really born again until the Holy Spirit leads us through conviction to the place where we're fed up with worshiping things or people. We must come to the realization that we need something better, and we must understand what that something better is so that we can make an intelligent choice. First, the Spirit convicts us of our need; second, He brings us to the point of conversion, or regeneration. Then we are ready for the new birth.

We had no choice in the matter of our first birth. Few would argue that point! And though our parents had a hand in making it happen,

God, the Author of life, is responsible for giving us our existence. Not only that, but God is directly responsible for keeping our hearts beating right now. He's the One who keeps us alive during our time here on earth, until we've used up whatever portion of those "threescore years and ten" that is our lot.

But while we had no choice in the matter of our first birth, God has made sure that we *do* have a choice in our second birth—in being born again. And the most complete description of this new birth is found in John, chapter 3. Let's focus on verses 3–5 (NIV).

Nicodemus, a member of the Jewish ruling council, had come for a secret interview with Jesus. The Savior cut right to the point of Nicodemus's need: " 'No one can see the kingdom of God unless he is born again.' "

Nicodemus replied, " 'How can a man be born when he is old? . . . Surely he cannot enter a second time into his mother's womb to be born!' "

Jesus said, " 'No one can enter the kingdom of God unless he is born of water and the Spirit.' "

It's interesting that Jesus Himself respected the Holy Spirit's timetable for bringing about the new birth. He didn't press Nicodemus or crowd him. Jesus didn't ask Nicodemus to be baptized next weekend. He simply gave Nicodemus a complete discourse on the subject of conversion and then left the Holy Spirit to do His work. For three years, Nicodemus waited and pondered. Outwardly, there was little change. But Jesus knew what He was doing, and eventually Nicodemus gladly surrendered and accepted Jesus as his personal Savior.

If you study John chapter 3 on Nicodemus and put it together with the next chapter, on the Samaritan woman at the well, then you'll come up with a four-part definition for conversion. First, it's a supernatural work of the Holy Spirit. Second, it produces a change of attitude toward God. Third, it gives us a capacity for knowing God that we didn't have before. And fourth, it leads to a new life of willing obedience to all of God's commands.

Notice, that conversion *leads* to a *willing* obedience, which is evidence that something has happened to change the inside. It's *not* a sudden resolution on the part of the sinner to clean up the outside. It's discovering that day by day our will is coming into harmony with God's will. And it's a process—not something that happens overnight!

TWO MISUNDERSTANDINGS

There are two misunderstandings that often lead to discouragement for those who've recently committed themselves to God. The first is the idea that conversion is an immediate, dramatic, total change of behavior. Often, when people have this idea and then discover that they're still facing some of the same temptations and tendencies and problems as they had before they were converted, they give up. They assume they weren't really converted after all and settle down to wait for the next evangelistic series, altar call, or whatever.

The second misunderstanding is to think that conversion is a one-time decision and that once we've made that commitment, we've made it for the rest of our lives. But conversion is a *daily* matter. We must seek the Lord and be converted every day. Only then will our murmurings be stilled, our difficulties be removed, and the perplexing problems we're facing be resolved.

Now, both of these mistaken ideas about conversion can be easily solved if we remember what conversion really is. Romans 12:2 tells us that it is the renewing of our *minds*. Ephesians 4:22–24 also speaks of this. Regeneration and renewal involve the thinking process. Conversion is not some magical behavior change that drops into our lives from above. Rather, it's the renewal of our ways of thinking, our attitudes. It's a continuing education in the things of Heaven. God never bypasses our minds in His dealings with us, for it is through our minds that we worship Him. Satan is the one who works by force, who doesn't really care what we think as long as we submit to his control. God wants only intelligent obedience and service.

By the way, this is a good principle to remember when you're seeking to recognize the true working of the Holy Spirit. If the focus is only on the outward behavior of the individual or the appeal is directed only at the emotions, then it's not God's approach. The Holy Spirit just doesn't work that way.

So, what *is* the primary means that the Holy Spirit uses to bring about this new birth? First Peter 1:23 gives us a clue: "You have been born again, not of perishable seed, but of imperishable, through the living and enduring word of God." In other words, the new birth takes place as the Holy Spirit works on our hearts through the messages found in God's Word. In addition, 2 Peter 1:4 points out that it is through God's Word that we "participate in the divine nature."

In God's Word, we find that Jesus died for us and now offers to take our sins and give us His righteousness. If we give ourselves to Him and accept Him as our Savior, then no matter how sinful our lives have been, for His sake we are counted righteous. Christ's character will stand in place of our character, and we are accepted before God just as if we'd never sinned. Isn't that good news! That's the assurance we have when we've been born again.

Remember, there is nothing *we* can do to save ourselves. And in spite of Jesus' great sacrifice, not everyone will be saved. Though His sacrifice was great enough for all, it's of no value to sinners until they *accept* it. And acceptance comes as the Holy Spirit helps us see our need, our helplessness, and our dependence upon God for salvation and brings us to the point of total surrender.

HOW THE NEW BIRTH HAPPENS

How does the new birth happen? Christ is constantly working upon the heart. Little by little, perhaps unconsciously to the receiver, impressions are made that tend to draw the soul to Jesus. These may be from meditating upon Him, from reading the Scriptures, or by hearing God's Word from a preacher or believer. Suddenly, as the Spirit comes with a more direct appeal, the soul gladly surrenders to

Christ. Many call this sudden conversion, but it's really the result of long, patient wooing by the Spirit of God.

We cannot convert someone else, but we *can* join in the work of the Holy Spirit. How? First, by uplifting Jesus to those around us; second, by sharing the truths we've discovered in God's Word; and third, by encouraging those seeking for a deeper spiritual life to go where God's Word is being presented.

Have *you* ever been converted? Have you been converted *today*? You cannot be a living Christian unless you have a daily experience in the things of God. You must advance *daily* in the divine life, and as you advance, you must be converted to God *every day*!

"But," you say, "how can I know if I've really been converted?"

Let me share some thought questions that will help answer this question.

1. Is Jesus the Center of your life? First John 5:12 says, "He who has the Son has life; he who does not have the Son of God does not have life." That's pretty straightforward, isn't it? Sometimes it's easy to say we love Christ when someone asks, but the real test is how much time we spend in His presence. If Jesus is the Center of our life, then everything we do will revolve around our relationship with Him. He'll be the first One we turn to for companionship; the last One for whom we can't find time. Who do *you* love to talk and think about most?

2. Do you have a deep interest in God's Word? First Peter 2:2 tells us that just as newborn babies crave milk, so should we desire the spiritual milk of God's Word. Until we're born again, it's an uphill battle to spend time seeking spiritual nourishment. But one of the first things that happens to people who've been born again is that they get hungry! And a new capacity for knowing God is one of the gifts the Spirit brings in His miracle of new birth.

3. Do you have a meaningful prayer life? " 'Now this is eternal life: that they may know you, the only true God, and Jesus Christ, whom you have sent' " (John 17:3, NIV). A Christian who is truly born again will have an earnest desire to communicate with God and with His Son, Jesus. Prayer is the breath of the soul, and it's essential that we breathe after we are born. Spiritually or physically, life without breath is extremely short!

4. Do you have a daily experience in the things of God? Luke 9:23 reminds us that if anyone wants to follow Christ, he must deny himself and take up his cross daily. The Christian life is not restricted to attending church a couple of hours each week. It's a *lifestyle*—a daily and hourly walk with God.

This chapter is taken from Morris Venden's book It's Who You Know *(Gentry, Ark.: Concerned Communications, 1996). Used by permission.*

Chapter 4

A REMARKABLE CONFESSION

CARLYLE B. HAYNES

This chapter is extracted from a sermon that Carlyle B. Haynes, a well-known Seventh-day Adventist evangelist, preached on July 11, 1926, during a General Conference session. After years of preaching, Haynes reached a point of total despair about his own spiritual experience. He said he hoped other people wouldn't have to go through what he experienced, but if they needed it, they must have it, however painful it might be. His striking testimony regarding the doctrine of justification by faith is very helpful to anyone interested in understanding and experiencing conversion.

I have been in this message about a quarter of a century. I started out to preach it nearly twenty-one years ago, and I have been preaching it without a break ever since. As most of you know, my work has been the public presentation of the teachings of the threefold message in various cities of the east and the south. I accepted the message with a very earnest, fervent sincerity. I believed in it, as I do now, with all my heart, and I gave to it all the energies of my life. I studied for a number of years what seemed to me to be the best method of presentation and of convincing speech. In my ministry, by the help of God, I was able to convince people of the truth of the great message that I believed—not only convince them, but they were persuaded, many of them, to unite with our churches and join us in this movement.

In those years of activity and of preaching the message here and there, I felt that the most important thing I could learn would be a convincing presentation of the message of God. I studied, therefore, not only to familiarize myself with all the teachings of the prophecies and the great doctrines, but also how to meet objections, how to answer questions, and how to remove from the minds of others anything that would be against their acceptance of this message as the truth.

During those years of preaching, at least during the earlier years of my ministry, my standing with God never concerned me very much. There were times when I would think of it, but not in any seriousness or for any length of time. I believed, when I thought of it at all, that everything must be all right between me and God because I was engaged in His service—I was doing His work, I was preaching His message and bringing people to believe it and accept it and come in with it. They were years of great activity, and the activity itself crowded out of my mind any conscious sense of my own personal need. I went on preaching with greater or less success. I found that I had a degree of convincing speech and an earnestness of presentation that persuaded men to believe what they were told. It seemed to me that God accepted me, and that my hope of eternal life was based on absolute assurance. I was preaching the second coming of Christ to others, and I thoroughly expected to meet Christ in peace when He came.

Some eight or ten years ago, I became concerned regarding my own experience in Christ. I found that the preaching of the prophecies of Daniel, the explaining of the 1,260 years, the 2,300 days, the truth of the Sabbath, the signs of Christ's coming, and the preaching of the unconscious state of the dead, had nothing in it—at least, the way I was doing it—that enabled me to conquer my own rebellious will or that brought into my life the power to overcome temptation and sin. I became somewhat concerned, and there was pressed into my conscience the question as to whether I really was accepted of God.

I reviewed my seeming success. I looked back over the experience that God had given me, and I was inclined to conclude again that, because of what I had done and was doing, I was safe. I tried to dismiss the questions that pressed themselves upon me in connection with my defeat when sin overcame me. But I could not dismiss them. They pressed upon me harder and harder. I then felt that the thing to do was to throw myself with new energy and more ardent endeavor into the preaching of the message. I became more rigid in my adherence to the faith. I straightened up some things in connection with my observance of the Sabbath. There were some things that I had allowed myself to do on the Sabbath that I quit doing. I was a little more scrupulous in my obedience to God. I preached with greater energy. I threw myself into all the activities of the ministry, hoping that by so doing, I would find the peace that I had once had, and dismiss and drive out of my heart the fears that were taking possession of me with regard to my own standing before the Lord. But the harder I worked, the more this thing troubled me. . . .

Defeated again and again

My activities didn't help me in any way. They but brought me into greater difficulty, for I found that I had no power in my life to oppose all the temptations of the devil, and that again and again and again, I was defeated. That question of personal victory—the lack of it in my life, and the need of it—began to burn in my soul, and there was a time when I questioned whether there was power in the three-fold message to enable a man to live a victorious experience in Christ Jesus. And I came into great trouble—so great that I cannot describe it to you adequately. But I was finally brought by this spiritual distress to a place where it was good for me to be, but where I hope I shall never be again—face to face with the profound conviction that, preacher as I was, and had been for fifteen years, I was lost, completely lost. I shall never forget my distress of mind and heart. I didn't know what to do. I was doing everything I knew how to do. I had made a supreme effort to live as I thought God wanted me to live; I was not doing anything consciously or intentionally wrong; but in spite of it all, the conviction came that I was lost in God's sight. And very nearly I felt that there was no way of salvation.

But through the mercy of God and the blessing of the Spirit, who never brings us to such a place but what He desires to carry us beyond that place, I was suddenly awakened to the fact that in all my connection with God and His work, I had neglected the first simple childlike step of coming to Jesus Christ for myself and, by faith in Him, receiving pardon for my own sins. All through those years, I *hoped* that my sins were forgiven, but I never could feel sure of it. God brought me back, after fifteen years of preaching this message, to the foot of the cross, and there came to me the realization of the awful fact that I had been preaching for fifteen years and yet was an unconverted man. I hope you don't have such an experience. But if you need it, oh, I hope you get it!

I made up my mind that I could take no further risk in a matter of such supreme importance. I came to Christ just as if I had never known Him before, as though I were just beginning to learn the way to Christ— as I was, in reality. I surrendered my sins to Jesus Christ, and by faith I received His forgiveness. And I am not in any confusion about that matter now!

I found that something else was necessary. I had the same old problems; the same passions, appetites, lusts, desires, inclinations, and dispositions; the same old will. I found it necessary to abandon myself— my life, my body, my will, all my plans and ambitions—to the Lord Jesus, and to receive Him altogether—not merely as the Forgiver of my sins, not merely to receive His pardon, but to receive *Him* as my Lord, my Righteousness, and my very Life.

I learned the lesson that the Christian life is not any modification of the old life. It is not any qualification of it, any development of it, not any progression of it, any culture or refinement or education of it. It is not built on the old life at all. It doesn't grow from it. It is entirely another life—a new life altogether. It is the actual life of Jesus Christ Himself in my flesh. And God has been teaching me that lesson. I don't think I have learned it altogether yet, but there is nothing on earth I want to learn so much as that. Years ago, I used to browse around in old bookstores and seize upon dusty old historical books as supreme treasures, trying to find something that would throw light on some dark prophecy. Today, while I am no less interested in the prophecies, I am much more interested in my union with Jesus Christ, and in the development and growth and progress of His life in me. . . .

Becoming a Christian, then, is not the acceptance of a body of teaching, nor a mental assent to a set of doctrines, nor believing the truth of the Bible in a mere intellectual way. It is not joining the church and partaking of the ordinances. It is entering into a new personal relation to Christ.

The inmost central glory of the gospel, therefore, is not a great truth, nor a great message, nor a great movement, but a great Person. It is Jesus Christ Himself.

Without Him, there could be no gospel. He came, not so much to proclaim a message, but rather that there might be a message to proclaim. He Himself was, and is, the Message. Not His teachings but Himself constitutes Christianity.

This chapter has been taken from a tract titled "Righteousness in Christ," written by Carlyle B. Haynes and published by the Ministerial Association of the General Conference of Seventh-day Adventists, as quoted by Norval F. Pease in his book By Faith Alone *(Mountain View, Calif.: Pacific Press®, 1962).*

Chapter 5

THE REGENERATING WORK
OF THE HOLY SPIRIT

R. A. TORREY

The following chapter is taken from an outstanding book by R. A. Tor-rey entitled The Holy Spirit: Who He Is and What He Does. *Here again we see what takes place in the new birth, how to experience it, and how to help others do the same. This chapter also includes the baptism of the Holy Spirit and the steps to receiving it. It makes a strong case for the necessity of the new birth.*

Previously, we studied the work of the Holy Spirit in convicting men of sin. We saw that it was the work of the Holy Spirit to convict them of sin and of righteousness and of judgment. Now, we shall study further the work of the Holy Spirit.

Jesus said, "When the Comforter is come, whom I will send unto you from the Father, even the Spirit of truth, which proceedeth from the Father, he *shall bear witness of me:* and ye also bear witness because ye have been with me from the beginning" (John 15:26, 27).* Here we see that *it is the work of the Holy Spirit to bear witness concerning Jesus Christ.* All the work of the Holy Spirit centers in Jesus Christ. It is His work to magnify Christ to us, *to glorify Christ* by taking of the things of Christ and declaring them unto us (cf. John 16:14).

---

* All Scripture in this chapter is quoted from the American Standard Version. All emphasis in the Scripture quotations used in this chapter has been added.

It is only through the direct testimony of the Holy Spirit in the individual heart that any man ever comes to a true and living and saving knowledge of Jesus Christ (cf. 1 Corinthians 12:3). No amount of listening to the testimony of men regarding Jesus Christ, and no amount even of studying what the Scriptures have to say about Christ Jesus will ever lead anyone to a true and living and saving knowledge of Jesus Christ unless the Holy Spirit, the living Spirit of God, takes the testimony of men, or takes the testimony of the Written Word, and interprets it directly to our hearts.

It is true that the Holy Spirit's testimony regarding Jesus Christ is found in the Bible. In fact, that is exactly what the whole Bible is—the Holy Spirit's testimony to Jesus Christ. The whole testimony of the Book centers in Jesus Christ. As we read in Revelation 19:10, "*The testimony of Jesus* is the spirit of prophecy." But while that is true, unless the living Spirit, who lives and works today, takes His own testimony as it is found in the Written Word, the Bible, and interprets it directly to the heart of the individual and makes it a living thing in the heart of the individual, he will not come to a real, living, saving knowledge of Jesus Christ.

If, therefore, you wish men to get a true view of Jesus Christ, such a view of Him that they will believe on Him and be saved, you must seek for them the testimony of the Holy Spirit, and you must put yourself in such relations to God that the Holy Spirit can bear His testimony through you. No amount of mere argument and persuasion on your part will ever bring anyone to a living knowledge of Jesus Christ.

And if you wish to have a true knowledge of Jesus Christ yourself, it is not enough that you study the Word and what the Spirit of God has said about Jesus Christ in the Word. You must seek for yourself the testimony of the Spirit of God directly to your own heart through His Word and put yourself in such relation to God that the Holy Spirit can bear His testimony directly to your heart. The attitude that you must take toward God in order that the Holy Spirit may bear His testimony to Jesus Christ directly to your heart is the attitude of absolute surrender to the will of God, for Peter is recorded as saying, "We are witnesses of these things; and so is the Holy Spirit, *whom God hath given to them that obey him*" (Acts 5:32). And we read these words of our Lord Jesus Himself in John 7:17, "If any man *willeth to do his will*, he shall know of the teaching, whether it is of God, or whether I speak from myself."

This explains why it is that one may read the Gospel of John time and time again and not come to a saving knowledge of Jesus Christ, even though that Gospel was written for the specific purpose of bringing men to a saving knowledge of Jesus Christ. The writer himself tells us in the twentieth chapter and the thirty-first verse, "These are written, that ye may believe that Jesus is the Christ, the Son of God; and that believing ye may have life in his name." But if the same man will surrender his will to God before beginning to read the Gospel, and will ask God each time he reads to send His Holy Spirit to interpret to his heart the things that he reads, he cannot read the Gospel through even once, without coming to believe that Jesus is the Christ, the Son of God, and through believing "have life in his name."

I have seen this illustrated many a time. One Sunday night as I was going out of the inquiry meeting in the Moody Church, a young man was waiting for me in the vestibule. I think he had already been a church member. He said to me, "Mr. Torrey, I don't believe anything. Can you tell me how to believe?"

"Don't you believe anything at all? Don't you believe there is a God?"

"Yes," he said. "I believe there is a God, but I am in doubt about everything else."

"All right," I said. "If you believe there is a God, you ought to surrender your will to God. Then begin at the first chapter of John, first verse, read a few verses at a time, not too many, and pay close attention to what you read and each time before you read, pray this prayer, 'Oh God, show me what of truth there is in these verses I am about to read, and what Thou showest me to be true I promise to take my stand upon.' And read on day after day consecutively until you get through the Gospel. Will you do it?"

"Yes," he replied, "I will."

"One thing more, when you get through the Gospel, come and report to me."

About two weeks after, when I went out of prayer meeting one night, I met him in the vestibule again. He said, "I have come to report."

I said, "What is your report?"

He said, "Don't you know?"

"Yes," I replied, "I think I do."

"Well," he said, "my doubts are all gone. I do believe that Jesus is the Christ, the Son of God, and I do believe in the Bible as the Word of God."

Why did he now believe when he didn't believe before, although he had read the same book through time and time again? He believed now because he had put himself in such a relation to God that the Holy Spirit could bear His testimony through His own Written Word.

THE SPIRIT'S OWN TESTIMONY

This story also explains why it is that one who has been long in the darkness concerning Jesus Christ so quickly comes to see the truth when he surrenders his will to God. It explains an experience that pretty much every thoughtful worker has had: You sit down beside an inquirer who really desires to know the truth and be saved, and you take your Bible and show him from some of the plainest statements of the Word just what one must do to be saved, namely, to believe on Jesus Christ; and you take the truth about Jesus Christ's atoning death and about His resurrection, and about His being a deliverer from the power of sin today, and you show it to him from some of the plainest statements of the Bible along those lines; and you make the way of life as plain as day, and you go over it, and over it, and over it; but still the inquirer does not see it at all but sits there dumb, puzzled, perplexed, bewildered, and he very likely tells you, "I cannot see it," yet you have made it as plain as day. That is, to you it is as plain as day. But it is not plain to him, and sometimes you are tempted to think that the inquirer is intellectually stupid. Not at all. He is perfectly clear about other things. And then you go on and on, and you go over it again and again, and suddenly a new light comes into the inquirer's face and he exclaims, "I see it—I see it," and he believes on Jesus Christ and is saved right then and there. Now what has happened? Simply this: the Holy Spirit has borne *His* testimony directly to that inquirer's heart.

So in all our dealing with inquirers, we must not only make sure that we give them the right Scripture to show them that they need a Savior and that Jesus Christ is just the Savior they need, *we must see to it also that we are looking to the Spirit of God to bear His witness to Jesus Christ* through us and that we are in such a relation to God that the Holy Spirit can bear His witness to Jesus Christ through us.

Take what occurred on the Day of Pentecost. The apostle Peter bore his testimony to Jesus Christ and gave the testimony of the Old Testament Scriptures, and the Holy Spirit, through Peter's testimony and that of the Old Testament Scriptures, bore His testimony to Jesus Christ, and so men saw and believed, and in that day "there were added unto them about three thousand souls." Now, if the apostle Peter had given just the same testimony the day before and had given just the same Scriptures the day before (that is, the day before Pentecost—the day before the Holy Spirit was given), there would have been no such results. But the time had come for the Holy Spirit to do His work, and Peter had been "filled with the Holy Spirit" "when Pentecost was fully come," and now not only did Peter give his testimony, but *the living Spirit of God,* who had taken possession of Peter, *gave His testimony,* and men saw and believed.

Mr. Moody used to put it in this graphic way. He said, "Peter said, 'Let all the house of Israel therefore know assuredly, that God hath made him both Lord and Christ, this Jesus whom ye crucified' (Acts 2:36), and the Holy Spirit said, 'Amen,' and men saw and believed."

At one time when I was superintendent of the Bible Institute in Chicago, I lived in the Bible Institute. Every night I would try to get home from my own meetings before the students got home from the various places they had gone to help in the work. I would meet them on the stairway and we would talk over the experiences of the night together.

One night a large company of them came back from the Pacific Garden Mission, full of enthusiasm and joy. "Oh," they said, "Mr. Torrey, we had a wonderful time at the Pacific Garden Mission to-night. Crowds of men came to the altar, all kinds of drunkards and outcasts, and were saved." The next day I met Harry Monroe, who was at that time in charge of the Pacific Garden Mission. I said, "Harry, the boys tell me you had a wonderful time at the Pacific Garden Mission last night." He replied, "Mr. Torrey, do you want to know the secret of it? I just held up Jesus Christ, and it pleased the Holy Spirit to illumine the face of Jesus as I held Him up, and men saw and believed." I thought that was a beautiful way of putting it.

So when you and I preach, or when we do personal work or teach, we should hold up Jesus Christ as He is presented in the Scriptures and then look to the Holy Spirit to illumine His face. And we should be very sure we are in such a relation to God and to the Holy Spirit and so dependent upon the Holy Spirit and so counting upon the Holy Spirit to do His work that He can do it, and then men will see and believe.

Let me repeat it in order that we may be sure that you get it: if you wish men to see the truth about Jesus Christ, do not depend upon your own powers of expression or persuasion or upon your own knowledge of Scripture and just how to use it, but cast yourself upon the Holy Spirit in a realization of your utter helplessness, and look to Him to bear His testimony to Jesus Christ, and see to it also that those you are dealing with put themselves in such an attitude toward God that the Holy Spirit can testify to them, and see to it also that you are in such a relation to God—so fully surrendered to Him, so separated from all that hinders His work—that He can bear His testimony through you. In the Holy Spirit's testimony to Jesus Christ lies the cure for all ignorance concerning Christ, and all skepticism concerning Christ.

REGENERATION

Now let me call your attention to another wonderful, gracious, and glorious work of the Holy Spirit.

Jesus answered and said unto him [that is, unto Nicodemus], Verily, verily, I say unto thee, Except one be born anew [or "from above"], he cannot see the kingdom of God. Nicodemus saith unto him, How can a man be born when he is old? can he enter a second time into his mother's womb, and be born? Jesus answered, Verily, verily, I say unto thee, Except one be *born of* water and *the Spirit,* he cannot enter into the kingdom of God! (John 3:3–5).

Here we are told that men are *born of the Spirit, or born anew through the Holy Spirit's power.* Exactly the same truth is set forth in Titus 3:5, in a way that may enable you to grasp it more readily: "Not by works done in righteousness, which we did ourselves, but according to his mercy he saved us, through the washing of regeneration and *renewing of the Holy Spirit."* Here we are taught that *it is the work of the Holy Spirit to renew men, or to make men anew—or, to use the common theological expression, to regenerate men.*

What is *regeneration?* We have two definitions of *regeneration,* or the new birth, in the Bible. You will find the first of these definitions in Ephesians 2:1, "You did he *make alive,* when ye were dead through your trespasses and sins." *Regeneration is, then, the impartation of life to men who are morally and spiritually dead because of their trespasses and sins.* Every man and woman and child of us, no matter how excellent in character or how religious our parents may have been, was born into this world spiritually dead. We are by nature moral and spiritual corpses. In regeneration, we are made alive; God imparts to us His own life. It is the Holy Spirit by whom God imparts to us this life. Regeneration is His work.

Of course, the Word of God is the instrument that the Holy Spirit uses in imparting life. We are taught that in 1 Peter 1:23, "having been begotten again, not of corruptible seed, but of incorruptible, through the word of God, which liveth and abideth." And we are told the same thing in James 1:18, "Of his own will he brought us forth by the word of truth, that we should be a kind of firstfruits of his creatures."

We see plainly in both of these passages that the Word of truth, the Word of God, the Word contained in the Bible, is the instrument that the Holy Spirit uses in regeneration, *but it is only as the Holy Spirit uses the Word that regeneration results.* The mere Written Word will not produce the new birth, no matter how faithfully preached or faithfully given in personal work, unless the living Spirit of God makes it a living thing in the hearts of those to whom we preach or with whom we are dealing.

This truth comes out very plainly in another statement of the apostle Paul's, found in 2 Corinthians 3:6, "The letter killeth, but the *Spirit giveth life.*" What does this mean? It is often taken in these days of superficial and careless thinking and careless Bible study to mean that the literal interpretation of Scripture, which these men call "the letter," that is, taking the Scripture to mean just what it says by applying the usual laws of grammar and diction, kills, but that some spiritualizing interpretation, some interpretation that makes the Word mean something it evidently was not intended to say, gives life. This is one of the favorite tricks in misinterpreting the Scriptures employed by those who are determined not to take the Bible as meaning what it says; and they call all those of us who insist on interpreting the Bible to mean what it says "deadly literalists." There never was a more unwarranted misconstruction of Paul's words—or the words of anyone else—than that. Paul did not have the remotest thought of teaching anything of that kind. If there ever was a "deadly literalist" (if literalism is really deadly), it was the very man who wrote these words. Paul was always insisting upon the exact force of every word used. Paul would build a whole argument on a word, or on a part of a word, on the number of a noun, or on the case of a noun, or on the tense of a verb. No, Paul did not mean anything of that kind.

What did he mean? Well, the way to discover what any man really means by what he says or writes is to *read what he says or writes in the connection in which it is said.* In this case, the connection shows beyond the possibility of honest doubt exactly what Paul meant. In the third verse of this same chapter, Paul draws a contrast between, on the one hand, the Word of God written on parchment or on paper with pen and ink or graven on tables of stone as in the case of the Ten Commandments, and, on the other, *the Word of God written,* as he puts it, *by "the Spirit of the living God;* not in tables of stone, but *in tables that are hearts of flesh."* What Paul, therefore, says is that the mere "letter" of the Word—the Word written or printed in a book—kills. In other words, it brings condemnation and death. But the Word of God *written by the Spirit of the living God in our hearts* ("in tables that are hearts of flesh") brings life.

This, of course, is only to say in other words what we have already said above, that *it is only as the living Holy Spirit takes today to the heart of the individual the Word of God and writes it on the heart* that men are made alive, or born again. No amount of giving the Bible, the Written Word, in sermon, or personal work, or teaching, will ever lead to a man being born again. If we wish to see men born again through our preaching, or through our personal work, or through our teaching, we must realize our dependence upon the Holy Spirit and look to Him and count upon Him to carry home to the heart the truth that we preach or give out in personal work or in teaching. And we must see to it that we ourselves are in such a relation to God that the Holy Spirit can do His regenerating work through us.

A SECOND DEFINITION

We have a second God-given definition of regeneration in 2 Peter 1:3, 4, "His divine power hath granted unto us all things that pertain unto life and godliness, through the knowledge of him that called us by his own glory and virtue; whereby he hath granted unto us his precious and exceeding great promises; that through these ye *may become partakers of the divine nature,* having escaped from the corruption that is in that world by lust." *God's definition of regeneration here is the impartation of a new nature, "the divine nature"—God's own nature—to us.*

We are all born into this world with a corrupt nature, corrupt in its thoughts, corrupt in its affections, corrupt in its will.

All of us, no matter how fine our ancestry or how pious our parents, are born into this world with a mind that is blind to the truth of God. As Paul puts it in 1 Corinthians 2:14, "The *natural man* receiveth not the things of the Spirit of God: *for they are foolishness unto him; and he cannot know them,* because they are *spiritually judged.*"

All of us born into this world with affections that are corrupt—that is, with affections set upon things that displease God. We love the things we ought to hate, and we hate the things we ought to love.

All of us born into this world with a will that is perverse. As Paul puts it in Romans 8:7, "*The mind of the flesh* [that is, the mind of the natural and unregenerate man] *is enmity against God;* for it is not subject to the law of God, neither indeed can it be." We are all of us born into this world with a will that is perverse, a will that is set upon pleasing self and not set upon pleasing God.

Now, what pleases self may not be something corrupt or criminal or vile or immoral. What pleases us may be something refined, something of a high character; it may not be getting drunk or stealing or lying or committing adultery or doing any evil or vile or base thing. It may be culture or music or art or some other high and refined thing; but *pleasing self is the very essence of sin,* whether the thing that pleases self is something very high or something very low. And any will that is set upon pleasing self is a will in rebellion against God; it is "enmity against God." There is only one right attitude for the human will, and that is an attitude of absolute surrender to God, and the whole aim of life should not be to please self at all but to please God in all things.

So then we are all born into the world with this nature that is intellectually, affectionally, and volitionally corrupt. What occurs in the new birth? We are given a new nature.

1. We are given a new intellectual nature, a new mind, a mind that instead of being blind to the truth of God is open-eyed to the truth of God. How often I have seen that. I have seen a man come into a meeting an utter infidel. I have a man in mind at this moment, a man who had not been inside a church for fourteen years and who was a rank and very bitter infidel. But this man was induced to come and hear me preach. The Spirit of God wrought through me that night and through a personal worker who dealt with him in the after-meeting, and that man was born again then and there, and that thoroughly darkened mind became illuminated at once, and, instead of the things "of the Spirit of God" being any longer "foolishness unto him," they became as clear as day, and within a week, he was bringing others into a knowledge of the truth. He brought his own wife to meeting the following Sunday night and led her into the light, and within a year, he was preaching the gospel.

2. We are not only given a new intellectual nature, we are also given a new affectional nature. We get new tastes instead of the old tastes, new loves instead of the old loves. Instead of loving any longer the things that displease God, we now love the things that please God. The things we once hated we now love, and the things we once loved we now hate. How clearly that was illustrated in my own experience. As I look back upon my life before I was born again, I can hardly believe what I know to be true about my own affections and about my likes and my dislikes before I was born again. In those days, I hated the Bible. I read it every day, but it was to me about the most stupid book I read. I would rather have read last year's almanac any day than to have read the Bible. But when I was born again, my heart was filled with love for the Bible, and today, I would rather read the Bible than any other book or all books put together. I so love it that sometimes I think I will not read any other book but the Bible. In those former days, before I was born again, I loved the card table, the theater, the dance, the horse race, the champagne supper, and I hated the prayer meeting and the Sunday services. Today, I hate the dance and the card table and the theater and the horse race, and I love the gathering together of God's people and the services of God's house on the Lord's Day. It is just as Paul puts it in 2 Corinthians 5:17, "If any man is in Christ, he is a new creature: the old things are passed away; behold, they are become new."

3. *In the new birth, we are not only given a new intellectual nature and a new affectional nature, we are also given a new volitional nature—that is, we are given a new will.* When one is born again, his will is no longer set upon pleasing self; his will is set upon pleasing God. There is nothing else in which he so delights as he delights in the will of God. What he himself desires is nothing to him; what pleases God is everything to him.

THE IMPARTATION OF GOD'S OWN NATURE

We see, then, that the new birth is the impartation of a new nature, God's own nature, to men who are dead in trespasses and sins. *It is the Holy Spirit who imparts this nature.* As we have already said, the Word of God is the instrument the Holy Spirit uses in imparting this new nature. This comes out in the very verse we have already quoted as containing God's definition of the new birth, 2 Peter 1:4, "He hath granted unto us *his precious and exceeding great promises; that through these* [that is, through *His precious and exceeding great promises*—that is, through the Written Word] ye may become partakers of the divine nature." Yes, always the Written Word is the instrument through which the new nature is imparted to men, *but it is only as the Holy Spirit uses the instrument, the Written Word, that the new birth—the impartation of God's own nature to us—results.*

So we see again that if we wish to be born again ourselves, it is not enough to read the Bible, though that is the instrument the Holy Spirit uses in regeneration. We must put ourselves in such an attitude toward God by the surrender of our will to God that the Holy

Spirit may use the Written Word and make it a living thing in our hearts and thus impart God's nature to us and thus we be born again. We see also that if we wish others to be born again through our preaching or personal work or teaching or whatever it may be, we must see to it that we not only give them the Written Word and give them the right passages from the Word, but also that we are in such a right relation toward God, and that we so realize our dependence upon the Holy Spirit for Him to do the work, and that we so count upon Him to do the work, that He can do His regenerating work through us.

The mere letter of the gospel will bring condemnation and death unless accompanied by the Holy Spirit's power. The ministry of many a perfectly orthodox preacher or teacher is a ministry of death; indeed, one of the deadest things on earth is dead orthodoxy. His ministry is a ministry of death because while he gives the Word, he gives it "in persuasive words of wisdom," but not "in demonstration of the Spirit and of power" (1 Corinthians 2:4). No amount of preaching, no matter how orthodox it may be, no amount of mere study of the Word will regenerate a person unless the Holy Spirit works. It is He and He alone who makes a man a new creature. But, thank God, He is ever ready to do this when the conditions are supplied that are necessary if He is to do His work. We are all dependent upon Him if there are to be real results, real regeneration.

Just as we are utterly dependent upon the work of Christ *for* us in justification, so *we are utterly dependent upon the work of the Holy Spirit in us for regeneration.* The whole work of regeneration can be described in this way: the human heart is the soil, the Word of God is the seed, and we preachers and teachers and personal workers are the sowers. We go to the granary of the Bible and take from it that portion of seed we wish to sow, and we preach it or teach it or use it in personal work. But if it all stopped there, no real result would follow—there would be no new birth. But if, as we preach or teach or do personal work, we look to the Holy Spirit to do His work, He will quicken the seed as we sow it, and it will take root in the hearts of those to whom we speak, and the human heart will close around it by faith, and a new creation will be the result.

I am often asked if I believe in sudden conversion. I believe in something far more wonderful than sudden conversion—I believe in sudden regeneration. Conversion is an outward thing; it means merely turning around: one is faced one way—faced away from God; he turns around and faces the other way—he faces toward God. That is conversion. But regeneration goes down to the very depths of the human heart and spirit. It is a radical transformation of the innermost man, an impartation of life, and the impartation of a new nature. An outward conversion, if it is to be real and lasting, must be the result of an inward regeneration. A man may be converted a hundred times, but he cannot be born again but once; for, when one is born again, when God imparts His own nature to a man, he stays born again. As John puts it in 1 John 3:9, "Whosoever is begotten of God doeth no sin [that is, not making a practice of sin], because *his seed* [that is, God's seed; God's own nature] *abideth in him:* and he cannot sin [that is, making a continuous practice of sin], because he is begotten of God." Yes, I believe in sudden regeneration—a sudden, thorough transformation of the inmost man.

WHY I BELIEVE IN REGENERATION

Why do I believe in it? Because God's Word teaches it, and because I have seen it over and over again. How could I doubt it when I had sitting beside me week after week and year after year on the platform of the Moody Church in Chicago as my assistant pastor a man who, up to the time he was forty-two years of age, was one of the most desperate and notorious sinners who ever lived, a man who at the age of nine was a drunkard and who was utterly incorrigible all through his school days. A man who entered the United States Navy at the age of fifteen and went through the Civil War and learned all the vices of the Navy and who at the close of the war went into the regular army and learned all the vices of the army and spent a good deal of that time while with the army at Fort Leavenworth in the guardhouse and was there elected the leader of a gang of desperados who were confined in the army guardhouse at that time. A man who was ordered out of the city of Omaha by the mayor and chief of police for almost killing the bully of Omaha in a fight. A man who rode down the streets of Omaha in a cab with a revolver in each hand, firing the revolvers out of both windows as he sped down the street. A man who, in spite of the money he inherited from his father, was outlawed from the town where he lived in Iowa, but who came back to that same town one night, went into a gospel meeting, and knelt at the altar and accepted Jesus Christ and was transformed into the best friend I ever had in my life. A man I loved as I never loved any other man. A man of whom if anybody should ask me who was the most Christlike man I ever met in my life, I would reply without hesitation, "Reverend William S. Jacoby"—the dearest man I ever knew. Yes, I believe in sudden regeneration.

If I didn't believe in sudden regeneration, I would quit preaching, for what would be the use of it all? What use, for example, of my preaching to such a congregation as I used to preach to every Sunday night in the Moody Church in Chicago, when that building was packed with the motley crowds who gathered there? Some of the finest Christians in Chicago were there; university students, medical students, law students, lawyers, doctors, and prominent businessmen and earnest Christian men and women were there. But "jailbirds," criminals just out of Joliet State Prison, infidels, outlaws, and depraved men of pretty much every nation on earth were there too. What would be the use of preaching to a crowd like that if it were not for the regenerating work of the Holy Spirit? But, believing as I did in the regenerating work of the Holy Spirit, I always arose to preach with a heart full of hope and expectation, for I never knew any night where the Spirit of God, God's holy Dove, would light.

Take, for example, one specific Sunday night. There had come into the audience that night, long before the meeting began, a man so intoxicated that the moment he was given a seat, he went to sleep. He wasn't turned out, for we had given our ushers instructions never to turn out any man no matter how drunk unless he insisted on making a disturbance, and, if they were compelled to turn a man out, to follow him out and deal with him, and, if possible, lead him to Christ. This man didn't make a disturbance, except possibly, he snored a little.

As I rose to preach that night, I offered a prayer before I preached, as I usually do. But I offered that night a different prayer from any I ever offered before, and I have never offered the same prayer but once since, and that was when this man asked me to offer it again. I am sure God put it on my lips that night, for I knew nothing about this man. The prayer I offered was this: "Oh God, if there is any man here in Chicago Avenue Church tonight who has run away from New York or from any other eastern city, and has left his wife and children there to starve, and is drinking himself to death here in Chicago, save that man tonight." Though I had never heard of this man before, that prayer described that man's case exactly. He had not only run away from an eastern city but from New York, and he had left his wife and children there to starve, and he was drinking himself to death in Chicago. Just as I offered that prayer, he awakened from his slumber, and he heard my words, and they sank into his heart. When he left that building, he could think of nothing else. As he afterwards described it to me and others, that night he wet his pillow with his tears, and God saved him. He got up a regenerated man. Dear man, how well I remember him! I can see his face yet.

THE BLACKLISTED ENGINEER

That very same night, there was a man sitting up in the gallery to my left who was a competent railroad engineer but who had been blacklisted by every railroad running into Chicago because of his intemperate habits. As I preached that night, the Holy Spirit carried my words home to that man's heart, and he believed on Jesus Christ and was saved and born again. As I finished preaching, one of my elders stepped up to him and said to him, "Are you saved?"

The man replied, "I am."

The elder said, "When were you saved?"

He said, "About five minutes ago as that man was preaching."

The next day, that man went down to the office of the vice president of the Chicago and Eastern Illinois Railroad. How an engineer who was blacklisted by every railroad running into Chicago ever got into the office of the vice president of the Chicago and Eastern Illinois Railroad, I do not know; but he certainly did. He said to the vice president, "I am a competent railroad engineer, but I have been blacklisted by every railroad running into Chicago for getting drunk. However, last night I was converted up in the Moody Church." The vice president sprang from the table, went to the door and locked it, and said, "I believe in that sort of thing. Let us pray." And so the vice president of the railway and the engineer who was blacklisted by every railroad running into Chicago knelt and prayed together. When they got up from the floor, the vice president said to him, "Everything I say on this road goes. I will give you a letter to the foreman of the roundhouse at Danville. He will give you an engine."

Oh, yes, I believe in sudden regeneration, and, believing in the regenerating power of the Holy Spirit through the Written Word—knowing that He has power to make men and women all over by quickening the words sown in the human heart, I never despair of any man or woman on earth, and I expect to keep on preaching and teaching the mighty Word of God in the power of the Holy Ghost as long as I have strength enough to stand on my feet and preach. Yes, if God sees fit to put me on a sickbed before I pass into eternity or before the Lord comes, I expect to preach Jesus Christ to men there on the sickbed in the power of the Holy Spirit, and I expect to see men and women and children born again. Is it any wonder that I wouldn't give up preaching the gospel to be president of the United States or to occupy any throne on earth?

This doctrine of the new birth is a glorious doctrine. It is true that it sweeps away false hopes. It comes to the man who is trusting in his morality and says, "Morality isn't enough. *You must be born again.*" It comes to the man who is trusting in reform, in turning over a new leaf, and says, "Reform is not enough, no matter how thorough it may be. *You must be born again.*" It comes to the man or woman who is trusting in education and culture and says, "Education and culture are not enough—*you must be born again.*" It comes to the man or woman who is trusting in his or her amiability of character, in his kindness of heart and generosity in giving, and says, "Amiability of character, kindness of heart, and generosity in giving are not enough. *You must be born again.*" It comes to the one who is trusting in the externalities of religion, in the fact that he goes to church regularly and has been baptized and united with the church, and partakes of the Lord's Supper, and regularly reads his Bible and says his prayers, and says, "All the externalities of religion are not enough. *You must be born again.*"

Yes, the doctrine of the new birth sweeps away all the false hopes that a multitude of churchgoers are building upon, and says there is a better way, the only way. While it sweeps away false hopes, it brings in a new, a better, a living hope. It comes to each and every one of us and says, *"You must be born again."* It comes to the one who has no taste for the things of God and therefore thinks there is no hope for him, and says, *"You may be born again."* It comes to the one who is down in sin of one kind or another, the one who is struggling hard but futilely to break away from sin, and says, *"You may be born again and lose all your love for sin and thus the power of sin be utterly broken."* It comes to the one who has wandered so far from God and committed so many sins that he thinks there is no hope for him . . . the one full of utter and hopeless despair, and says, *"You may be born again; you may be made all over; you may become a child of God and a partaker of His own holy and glorious nature."* Hallelujah!

Oh, men and women, have you been born again? I do not ask you whether you are church members. I do not ask whether you have been baptized. I do not ask whether you go regularly to the Lord's Supper. I do not ask you whether you are giving as much of your income to the church and to the poor as you should give. I do not ask you whether you go to prayer meeting regularly and say your own prayers regularly every day and study your Bible regularly. I ask you, *Have you been born again?* Have you become a partaker of God's own nature? If not, you may today. *The Spirit of God is able and He is ready to make you all over, to impart to you God's own nature through His Word if you will only let Him do it.*

This chapter was taken from R. A. Torrey's book The Holy Spirit: Who He Is and What He Does *(Grand Rapids, Mich.: Fleming Revell, 1927). Used by permission. (Under public domain.)*

Chapter 6

SIN RESULTS IN SINS

MORRIS VENDEN

The following chapter deals with one of the most important misunder-standings in the Christian world. Most people define sin in terms of be-havior, or doing bad things. This is not biblical at all, and we will en-deavor to correct this misunderstanding. In the process of doing so, we will also look at some of the devil's favorite Bible texts, which he has used to deceive and discourage millions. Then we will look at the wonderful per-spective on these texts that brings great relief and joy.

Did you ever have your head split wide open with a brand-new idea? It can be exhilarating. It can also be painful. What follows may seem to you like a brand-new idea, so give it a fair hearing.

I believe the devil has some favorite Bible texts. Don't you think the devil reads his Bible? I believe he has every version, and he knows all the texts that he can use to beat us over the head. I grew up with Revelation 3:5 haunting me: "He that overcometh, the same shall be clothed in white raiment; and I will not blot out his name out of the book of life, but I will confess his name before my Father, and before his angels."

Well, I liked the idea of having a white robe, whatever that means. I liked the idea of my name not being blotted out of the book of life. And it sounded good to have my name confessed before the Father and the angels. But obviously, according to the text, I had to over-come in order for that to happen. Right? And I wasn't doing very well. I was on the sawdust trail with my father and uncle, who were evangelists. I remember this text from my earliest childhood—"He that overcometh." I wanted to be an overcomer. I tried to overcome my sins. I tried to overcome fighting with my brother. It was usually his fault, but I wanted to be one of these overcomers. I heard about a group of people called the remnant who were supposed to be over-comers. And I wasn't making it. The harder I tried, the worse it got. And I fought with discouragement.

Then one day I discovered another one of the devil's favorite texts. It is found in Hebrews 10:26, 27, "If we sin wilfully after that we have received the knowledge of the truth, there remaineth no more sacrifice for sins, but a certain fearful looking for of judgment." And I knew that my sins were not all accidental. I had a Bible teacher who told us that there was no provision for deliberate sin in the Old Testament sacrificial system—only the kind you sort of fell into. So, this text left me out. Things began to look darker and dimmer for me and my eternal destiny. And the harder I tried, the worse it got.

I went to get some help from some of the good people. Like most people, I didn't start out by saying, "Look, I've got this problem." I asked the question in the third person: "What do you say when people ask you, 'How do I overcome?' " They said, "You have to remember James 4:7, 'Resist the devil, and he will flee from you.' " So I tried it. I had already tried it, but I figured I had better try harder. It didn't work. Every time I tried it, I got knots on my head. And I began to consider whether the Arminians were right or whether Calvin was right—whether everybody could be saved or whether some people were born to be fuel for the fires of hell, and I must be one of them.

In this discouragement, I discovered another one of the devil's favorite texts, Hebrews 12:4, "Ye have not yet resisted unto blood, striving against sin." I said, "Well, I guess that's my problem. I'm not trying hard enough. If I really get serious about this, I've got to resist unto blood. Then maybe I can become an overcomer."

I understood that prayer could help. And so I began to get serious about prayer. I decided I'd better pray more—at which point the devil led me to a couple more of his favorite texts: "Your iniquities have separated between you and your God, and your sins have hid his face from you, that he will not hear" (Isaiah 59:2). And then a first cousin of that text: "If I regard iniquity in my heart, the Lord will not hear me" (Psalm 66:18). So, I decided that I was so weak and so much in discouragement and failure that I had to have prayer. And then I discovered that God will not hear my prayers until I get rid of my iniquities. Isn't that clear? So I'm going to have to get rid of my iniquities so He can hear me. But I need Him to hear me in order to get rid of my iniquities.

Perhaps you've heard about the man whose car horn wouldn't work. He went downtown to a car repair shop, and the garage door was shut and there was a sign on the door that said, "Honk for service." So, he had a real problem. If you have to honk in order to have service and there is something wrong with your honker, you're going to be sitting there for a long time. If I have to get over my iniquities in order for God to hear me but I can't get rid of my iniquities until He hears me, I'm going to be sitting there for a long time.

I don't know if anyone else has been in the same shoes that I was wearing, but it was real. I can smile at it now, but when you feel that you are condemned and you're going to be lost and there is no hope for your eternal life because you can't be an overcomer and the devil is beating you over the head with these Bible texts, what can you do?

But you know something? God is good. He is kind. And He doesn't leave us alone. He will continue to stay with us and help us to understand until one day our head is split open with a brand-new idea.

HELP FROM A BOOK

Some time ago, I read a book on Galatians written by an Adventist preacher in the nineteenth century. I wish I could remember the name of the book and the name of the man who wrote it, but I can't. It wasn't by one of the well-knowns, such as Jones or Waggoner; it was by one of our less prominent pioneers.

The point is, this book introduced to me something I had never thought of before. Sin is not what we think it is. We think that sin is doing bad things. No, no, no. Doing bad things is the *result* of sin. Sin involves something far deeper than doing bad things. That Adventist pioneer began to open my eyes with Bible passages such as Romans 14:23, "Whatsoever is not of faith is sin." *Anything* I do—whether it's good or bad makes no difference—anything I do that I'm not doing through the life of faith is sin because I can only be doing it for selfish reasons.

That old preacher pointed me to John 16:8, 9, in which Jesus says that the Holy Spirit will come and will convict the world of sin, and then He tells us what sin is; the Spirit will convict the world "of sin, because they believe not on me." Sin consists of not having a trusting relationship with Jesus. That's what sin is. Then *sin* results in *sins*—doing wrong things. Suddenly, some things began to become clear to me.

Now, we must look at some definitions. *Sin* singular is separation from God. *Sin* singular is living life apart from God. We are called *sinners* because we are born separated from God. That's our problem. We didn't have to do any sinning in order to become sinners. All we had to do was to be born. Once we were born, we were sinners.

I was born of Norwegian and German heritages. I didn't have to do any "Norwegianing" and "Germaning" in order to be Norwegian and German. And you don't have to do any sinning to be born a sinner. All you have to do is to be born separated from God to be a sinner. And when you're a sinner, you do bad things—the things we usually call sins.

Well, when I learned that, I began to understand the point of lots of the Bible's stories and statements. The real issue in sin isn't the matter of doing bad things; it is living life apart from Jesus, thinking that we are strong enough to live on our own steam. If I have no time for God every morning—a text for the day with my hand on the doorknob, at best—then I'm living in sin regardless of how good or bad I am. What I do is beside the point.

Lucifer didn't fall because he stole mangoes off of the tree of life or broke others of the Ten Commandments in the usual classical ways. He fell because he decided he was big enough to separate himself from a relationship with his Maker. Sin is separation from God. When I learned that, suddenly, something my major professor used to tell us came clear. He used to say, "One of these days, there's going to be a great revival in the churches. It won't be based upon people getting up and confessing all of their terrible sins. No, it will be based upon the sudden realization that we have been living our spotless lives apart from Jesus. We have made a mistake. We have focused on behavior religion and behavior theology instead of relationship religion and relationship theology."

The relationship definition for sin is life lived apart from God—a broken relationship. What is God looking for in the whole controversy and the plan of salvation? He's looking for friends. He's looking for people who will come into close relationship with Him and depend upon Him, as He originally intended, and who stop living on their own steam. He has promised to take care of our sins if we do that. This is a major awakening.

I've discovered that this little topic is one of the most effective to help us get a clear picture of righteousness by faith, because once you get the issue of sin straight, everything else begins to fall into place. It's like when you come to a fork in the road. At first, starting down the wrong road may not take you very far from the right one. But eventually, you may end up all the way across the country from where you wanted to go. If you get the issue of what sin is straight to begin with, then the whole theme of salvation and righteousness by faith becomes clear.

A SECOND LOOK

Now, I'd like to show you how exciting it is when you get this straight and you begin to look at the same texts that the devil beat you over the head with. Suddenly, the devil meets himself coming back, and the texts that were threats become promises.

Let's go back and take a look at the first one, Revelation 3:5. This is exciting. "He that overcometh, the same shall be clothed in white raiment; and I will not blot out his name out of the book of life." "Overcometh" what? I used to think that I had to overcome my sins—my bad deeds. No! If the real issue in sin is living life apart from Christ, then this text is saying, "He that overcometh living life apart from Christ, the same shall be clothed in white raiment." It's a promise! He that overcometh living life apart from Jesus day by day won't have his name blotted out of the book of life. That makes all the difference in the world.

If Jesus asked us to promise never to do any sinning again, most of us would have to fall on our faces and say, "I'm in trouble. I'm in deep weeds." But if Jesus said, "Will you promise to enter into a relationship with Me? Can we get acquainted? Can we get to know each other?" then we're talking about something possible for the weakest sinner because Jesus knocks at the heart of every sinner, weak or strong, asking for entrance into fellowship and communion and relationship. That's what it's all about.

If that isn't what it's all about, or if it isn't doable, then the prophet of old was wrong when he said, "Thus saith the LORD, Let not the wise man glory in his wisdom, neither let the mighty man glory in his might, let not the rich man glory in his riches: But let him that glorieth glory in this, that he understandeth and knoweth me" (Jeremiah 9:23, 24). And Jesus was wrong when He said life eternal is about knowing "thee the only true God, and Jesus Christ, whom thou hast sent" (John 17:3). Now we're into relationship theology, where the important thing is who you know, and those people who worry about what they do don't have to worry because who you know has a lot to do with what you do. In fact, it's the only thing that has anything to do with what you do.

Strong people can produce outward righteousness. If we have a behavior-centered theology and a behavior-centered religion, then we're going to fill the church with strong people because they're the only ones who can meet the standards. The weak people who join the church soon discover that they can't measure up, and since they don't want to add hypocrisy to failure, they leave the church. But concerning these two groups, we need to remember that Jesus said the publicans and the harlots go into the kingdom before the best church members, the church leaders. Why? Because they realize their need of a relationship with God. Strong people don't. Strong people who can live a good moral life look into heaven and say, "God, take care of the sun, moon, and stars. Keep the planets from running into each other. And take care of the drunk in the gutter. But as for me, I'm doing fine, thank You. I don't need You." How do I know most professed Christians don't need Him? Because they have no time for Him day by day. And that identifies what sin is all about—the real issue in sin.

Well, when I began to realize this, I was on a roll. I decided to go and take a look at Hebrews 10:26, 27, and see how that came out with the new relationship definitions. "If we sin wilfully after that we have received the knowledge of the truth, there remaineth no more sacrifice for sins." What is this text saying? If I willfully live life apart from Jesus, after I know better, there's no more sacrifice for my sins. Well, the sacrifice is still there, but it's no good for me because the only way I continue to have His sacrifice covering my sins is to keep coming to Him day by day. So, if I have no time for Him because I'm too busy or I have more important things to spend my time on, like sports and TV, then I'm willfully living life apart from Him, I'm willfully sinning, and His sacrifice for my sins is not effective in my life. The issue is sinning willfully in terms of choosing to live life apart from Him.

Next I wondered about James 4:7, because the good people had really tried to work hard there. "Resist the devil, and he will flee from you." So, I went back and read it, and to my surprise, I realized that people have lifted the phrase right out of the middle of a passage. Why don't we try checking the context, for a change? Isn't that a novel idea! To my surprise, I found out that just before saying "resist the devil," the text says, "Submit yourselves therefore to God." That's relationship theology—submit yourselves to God! And right after the "resist the devil" line, in verse 8, the text says, "Draw nigh to God." So that line is surrounded by relationship factors.

I went to the good people, and I said, "Hey, why don't you read the whole text?"

"Oh," they said, "yes, we know we're supposed to have a relationship with God. Everybody knows that. But you've got to resist the devil. God doesn't do for you what you can do for yourself."

"COOPERATION THEOLOGY"

Have you ever heard this "cooperation theology"—"God helps those who help themselves"? I've found that God *doesn't* help those who help themselves. I believe the Bible teaching is that God helps those who *can't* help themselves. Not only that, but God helps those who can't help themselves and who *know* it. They're the ones that God can help. Only when we get to the end of our own resources can God move in with His power. Most of us waste our time and effort trying to get the victory when the crux of the matter is getting the victory over trying to get the victory.

Well, the good people said you have to draw nigh unto God and you have to resist the devil—both. I decided to ask the Greek experts about their interpretation. I studied Greek in college and seminary, and I learned enough Greek to know that I didn't know much Greek. You're not going to hear me bragging about my great Greek escapades. So, if I want to know about the Greek, I go to the experts.

I went to the Greek teachers, the experts, and I said, "Tell me about this one. What does it say here in James 4:7? Does it say that I am supposed to submit to God and draw nigh to God and then resist the devil too?"

They looked at it. They checked the construction. They checked the meanings of the original words. Then they said, "No. What it says here is that the way you resist the devil is by drawing nigh to God."

You don't resist the devil by trying to resist the devil. That led me into failure. The Greek experts said, "The way you resist the devil is by submitting to God." That's what it means.

My, I was getting excited now. And I thought, *Well, what about this text over in Isaiah that says that God won't hear me because of my iniquities?* I began to study the subject of prayer. And I discovered, to my surprise, that there are at least eight different kinds of prayer. Four kids of prayer are conditional and four of them are unconditional. So, yes, there are conditional prayers. Conditional prayers are the kind in which you ask God for special favors, such as sunshine and rain and prosperity. And there is plenty of Old Testament evidence that in matters of these special favors, such as prosperity, people forfeited God's blessing and He wouldn't hear them because of their sins.

But there are also unconditional prayers, and one of them is the prayer of a poor sinner who wants a relationship with God. God's answer to this prayer is unconditional. Any sinner who prays this prayer to Jesus is always, always heard and always, always accepted. So we better get it straight before we discourage people with the misuse of texts like this. I'm glad to know that sinners' cries for God are always heard.

Well, that led me to the final text that I thought told me to try to work harder and to resist more. That's the one in the twelfth chapter of Hebrews. Again, I had read one little verse, "Ye have not yet resisted unto blood, striving against sin" (verse 4). And I thought, *Why not read the context?*

Go back with me to the very beginning of Hebrews 12. Let's read the first three verses: "Wherefore seeing we also are compassed about with so great a cloud of witnesses, let us lay aside every weight [*every weight*], and the sin which doth so easily beset us"—I used to think this probably meant somebody's favorite sin. You know, we all have a favorite sin. Everybody is a sinner, but each of us has a dandy sin that we really love. So, we're supposed to lay aside this favorite sin.

No, *no*, NO! This text is talking about THE SIN.

What is THE SIN? Living life apart from God. That's the one.

The sin that doth so easily beset me is that of waking up in the morning when the pillow is soft and the bed is warm, and turning over and saying, "God, please accept the will for the deed. I will try to have time for You tomorrow, but I think I can live on my own steam today." Basically, I'm saying to God, "I'm big enough to face life today. You can take care of the drunks and the planets and just leave me alone. I'm doing fine." This is the sin that doth so easily beset me. This is the sin that doth so easily beset the pastor or the evangelist who is so busy doing the work of the Lord that he forgets the Lord of the work and the evidences of self begin to surface. This is the sin that doth so easily beset each of us.

The passage goes on to say, "Let us run with patience the race that is set before us, looking unto Jesus . . ."—now Jesus becomes the central focus of the passage—". . . looking unto Jesus, the author and finisher of our faith; who for the joy that was set before him endured the cross." And then verse 3 says, "For consider him [*consider him*] that endured such contradiction of sinners against himself, lest ye be wearied and faint in your minds. Ye have not yet resisted unto blood, striving against sin." As He did. Oh, Jesus becomes the focus, and He's the One who resisted unto blood, striving against sin.

I'm not going to make a case out of the wording of the King James Version, but it's very interesting: "striving against *sin*." What sin? What sin did Jesus strive against?

TEMPTED LIKE US

Now, I know that there are those who insist that Jesus had to struggle with every little thing that we ever struggle with. I have news for you. He was born two thousand years too early for that. I know there are people who say—they insist—that He was in all points, in every way, tempted like as we are. By the way, I checked with the experts on Greek regarding that, too, and the original reads, "He was tempted in all like as we are." The word *points* isn't there. He was tempted to every extent that we are. Tempted to do what? So, one day I decided to sit down and do a word study and find out just how much appeal sins had for Jesus.

So, I got out my CD-ROM. I got out my Bible. I checked the inspired writings. And I wrote page after page after page of single-spaced entries about how sins appealed to Jesus. *They had no appeal to Him whatsoever!* Zero. He was disgusted by sins. They were abhorrent to Him. And the Bible made that very clear. He "loved righteousness, and hated iniquity" (Hebrews 1:9). We can't say that about us. We're born wrong. But Jesus hated sins. In fact, I believe He hated them so much that they were no temptation to Him. I really believe that.

It's rumored that one of today's rock stars would pass a large cup up and down through the audience, and people would spit in the cup till it was overflowing. Then he would bring it up on the stage and drink it. I have news for you: don't try to tempt me with that one. Do you think I would have to use a lot of willpower and backbone to keep from doing that? Why, I'm so disgusted by the idea that victory over that temptation would be one of the easiest victories I ever got. That is the way sins appealed to Jesus. Zero. *Zero!* So, the devil knew he couldn't tempt Jesus to do wrong. He probably tried, but that's stupid when Jesus hates the sin. So, the devil had to tempt Jesus to do right.

Have you ever been tempted to do right? That's one of my biggest temptations. I wake up in the morning, and the pillow is soft and the bed is warm and I'm tempted to roll over and go back to sleep. I'm tempted to think I can do right that day in my own strength.

Jesus was tempted to turn stones into bread. There's nothing wrong with that when you're hungry, but He was tempted to do it in His own power. That's what the problem was. He was tempted to separate from His Father and depend upon Himself. This is what the devil tried to get Jesus to do all through His life.

Did Jesus have to struggle with that?

Of course He did. He was born God. Which means we don't have to worry about Him having every little point of temptation we have because He was tempted ten thousand times more than we will ever be on the real issue of sin, which is to separate oneself from God and live on one's own strength. So, those people who insist that Jesus had to be tempted on every little point we're tempted on are advertising that they're still stuck on behavior-centered theology. You see, the minute you shift into relationship theology, you are into the bigger issue, and Jesus becomes a greater Example to us on the real issue of sin.

"TRANSGRESSION OF THE LAW"

Well, this whole thing began to open up in such a way that it surprised me. I went to 1 John 3. You know what happens if you stand up in front of an audience of Adventists and you ask, "What is sin?" They'll say, " 'Sin is the transgression of the law' (1 John 3:4)—anything else you wanna know?" I grew up on that. It was a big surprise to discover that sin is *not* the transgression of the law. Transgression of the law is the *result* of sin.

I went to the Greek experts again, and I said, "Tell me what 1 John 3:4 says." They looked at it, and they read the whole thing. You know what it says—what it means? This is the meaning of 1 John 3:4: whoever commits sin, or lives life apart from God, transgresses *also* the law, for sin—living life apart from God—results in transgression of the law.

Here I'd been wasting my time and effort trying to get over transgressing the law when the real issue is overcoming living life apart from Him. Are you reading me? We waste our time and effort trying to become overcomers in the realm of behavior, and it's like putting Band-Aids on cancer. It doesn't work.

So we get back to the first text, Revelation 3:5, which discouraged me because I thought it said that only people who are about ready for translation could qualify for heaven. But Revelation 3:5 is for sinners. It says that if I will overcome living life apart from God, He will clothe me with white raiment. That's the way I get over my sins. And He has promised to do it. It's in the story of the man who went to the wedding without the wedding garment. In Revelation 19, being clothed in a white robe has to do with obedience, and it's a gift. Victory and overcoming and obedience are gifts from God, not something we work on or work up. This is good news for weak people. It's bad news for strong people because strong people get insulted. And when they discover that they're not going to get any credit for their years of hard work, they get mad about it. That's why at the very end, just before Jesus comes, many strong, stalwart church members will leave the church and many backsliders will return and take their place, because there is a new view of what the real issues are. All of this, of course, tells us that we need to make a decision. We need to decide to seek God as we have never sought Him before.

Jesus knew that experience, and He never deviated from it. In fact, the classic example of that experience in Jesus' life took place in Gethsemane. The devil knew that all through Jesus' life, he had tried to get Jesus to fall on the real issue—to ignore His trust in God, His dependence on Him, and to depend instead upon His own power, which He had plenty of.

Then Jesus comes to Gethsemane, and the devil isn't going to leave this matter of tempting Him to one of his lieutenants, he takes it on personally. As Jesus struggles with that strange thing we call the atonement, suddenly, it's like an angel of light shows up, if you please. It's the devil in disguise. And he says to Jesus, "Congratulations! You've done it well. All through Your life You've depended on Your Father. And You have never deviated from that. You've done a wonderful thing. Now, don't ruin it tonight. If You go through with this crucifixion, You're going to separate from Your Father, and that's what sin is all about." It was a clever maneuver. It was a reverse play.

But Jesus had done His homework. He knew about the process involved in the atonement. And three times He said, "God, please—I'm having a problem. I would just as soon not go through with this. It's too dark. It's too black." But He realized that you and I would need what He was doing that night. And though He fell dying to the ground, He said, "Not My will but Thine be done."

I've always been amazed at what happened then. An angel from heaven came with the speed of thought, if you please, arrived at the side of Jesus, lifted His head out of the dirt, cradled Him on his shoulder, pointed to the open heavens, and reminded Jesus that His Father was still bigger than the enemy and all of his forces. He told Jesus that what He was doing that night would result in millions of people being saved, eternally saved.

Jesus went through with it—for our sake. All He asks is that we spend some time with Him. Is that asking too much? What are your priorities?

Morris Venden prepared this chapter for this book.

Chapter 7

CONVERSION

MORRIS VENDEN

In this chapter, we will consider the steps that Inspiration indicates everyone takes in coming to Christ. They can be very helpful for those who want to know what is happening in their own lives or who are leading others to salvation.

Coming to Christ produces four results: God gives us repentance, we are justified (forgiven), the miracle of conversion takes place, and we begin a relationship with Christ. This relationship continues as long as we continue to seek Christ day by day through the Bible and through prayer. Our salvation experience then generates within us a desire to reach out to others in service—the third ingredient for a continuing relationship with Christ.

Everyone knows that if you want to go to sleep, there are a couple of things you should do. As a rule, you should put your back against a mattress. (Although I went to sleep once working on a combine harvester!) You should turn out the lights. You probably should turn your radio off too. And it helps to close your eyes!

When my daughter was small, I got into the bad habit of lying down with her until she went to sleep. Eventually, she wouldn't go to sleep until I would lie down with her. Sometimes I would have an appointment elsewhere, and I'd look out of the corner of my eye and say, "LuAnn, close your eyes." She would, but the next time I checked, they would be wide open again.

While you can't make yourself sleep, there are things you *can* do to make it more likely that you will go to sleep. Similarly, while you can't convert yourself, you *can* place yourself in the atmosphere where it can happen. You don't have to sit and wait forever for something to hit you.

If you are running from God but find that deep inside you want to come into the right relationship with Him, you can place yourself where the things of God are being presented. If you're a student on a campus where religious meetings are held, instead of skipping every meeting or trying to sleep or read your way through them, you can go and listen when the gospel is preached. If you consider the Bible a dull book and have let it gather dust on the shelf year after year, you can take a few minutes each day to consider deliberately some passage on the life of Jesus, inviting God to meet you where you are and to do His work in reaching your heart.

The responsibility for meaningful communication with God has to be *His,* not ours. But we can *come* to Him. We can place ourselves in an atmosphere where He can get through to us and then invite Him to work His miracle of regeneration in our lives. There are six steps that bring us to conversion.

STEP 1: DESIRE SOMETHING BETTER

Do you have a desire for something better than you presently know? If you do, it is God who gives you that desire. Whether or not you are ready to admit it, whether or not you'd identify the voice as coming from God, it is Him. He is drawing you. He is drawing your heart and your mind to Him.

"The first step toward salvation is to respond to the drawing of the love of Christ."[1] Everyone, everywhere, is being drawn—except possibly those who have already been brought to a confrontation with God and have turned Him down. Jesus said that the Holy Spirit

SIX STEPS TO CONVERSION

CONVERSION—a continuing experience
John 3:1–17
1 John 5:4, 5

STEP 6. **Repentance**—a gift, not a condition for acceptance with God
Acts 5:31
Luke 18:9–14

STEP 5. **Surrender**—not of sins but of self (of our efforts without God)
Romans 9:30–32
Romans 10:1–4

STEP 4. **Helplessness**—not worthlessness, but inability to change ourselves
Jeremiah 13:23
John 15:5

STEP 3. **Conviction** that we are sinners whether or not we've done wrong
John 16:8–10
Romans 3:10–12

STEP 2. **Knowledge** of God's love for humankind as revealed in the plan of salvation
John 5:39
Romans 10–17

STEP 1. **Desire** for something better, often sought through every way but God's
John 6:44
John 12:32

would " 'convince the world concerning sin' " (John 16:8, RSV). He didn't say the Spirit would convince only church members. And he didn't say just a few, but the whole world. Jesus also told us about His Father: "No man can come to me, except the Father which hath sent me draw him" (John 6:44). And Jesus Himself is involved, "I, if I be lifted up from the earth, will draw all men unto me" (John 12:32). The Three Mighty Persons of the Godhead are drawing all people to face the real issues of time and eternity and make their decisions.

Just becoming religious won't satisfy the desire God plants in your heart. There's a big difference between being religious and being spiritual. There's a difference between knowing the rules and knowing the Lord. There can be a big gap between going through the forms, playing the game called church, and really knowing God.

My telephone rang at 2:00 A.M. one morning. I stumbled down the hall to the phone and heard a woman's voice on the other end of the line. She said, "Sir, can you help me?"

I asked, "What kind of help do you need at this time of day?"

"I need to find God. Do you know God?"

Think for a moment of all the answers I could have given her. I could have said, "I'm a preacher," but she had asked, "Do you know God?"

"I studied Greek."

No. "Do you know God?"

"I keep the Sabbath and pay tithe."

"Sir, *do you know God?*"

That's the question each of us must answer. Do you know God? Do you know Him personally? That's your biggest need.

STEP 2: LEARN THE TRUTH ABOUT GOD

When we have responded to the God-given desire for something better, we must then learn what that something is. Knowledge—a correct knowledge of God and His love—is our second step in coming to Him.

If people receive their information about salvation from other people, there's a good chance they'll conclude that Christianity is based on behavior, because most people define it in terms of behavior. If you rely upon other people for your information, you're likely to end up with a misunderstanding of God.

"Study to shew *thyself* approved unto God" (2 Timothy 2:15; emphasis added). If you don't, you're going to be ashamed sometime. Study for *yourself*. Get the right knowledge for *yourself*. Don't depend upon what others tell you about God. Don't depend on the preacher. We have churches full of people today who are depending on the preachers for their information. God help them! The preacher may be just as wrong as the next person. You'd better find out for yourself what is right and what isn't.

Getting an accurate picture of God involves more than searching the Scriptures for information. The Jewish people of two thousand years ago did plenty of searching of the Scriptures, but they didn't find the One the Scriptures were intended to help them find. Don't read the Bible just for the sake of reading the Bible. Study for more than information. Study for communication. Don't pray just to get answers to your problems. Pray for communication.

"Seek, and ye *shall* find" (Matthew 7:7; emphasis added). Paul said we should seek God and find Him because He is "not far from every one of us" (Acts 17:27). God wants us to find Him. We aren't chasing down a God who is trying to elude us. We aren't looking for a God who is lost. We have a God who followed Adam when he hid in the Garden. A God who followed Jonah when he was deliberately running from his duty. A God who followed Saul of Tarsus as he fled from the stoning in Jerusalem that had brought conviction to his heart. It is only as we see the love of God for us that we'll be willing for Him to catch up with us.

When the devil sees us trying to gain a correct knowledge of God through the study of God's Word, he becomes nervous. As with every other step toward Christ, he has sidetracks designed to hinder us from reaching our goal.

Sometimes the devil can sidetrack people by getting them to start at the wrong place in the Bible. Is there a wrong place for a beginner to start? Have you become an authority on the book of Genesis because every year you've vowed to read your Bible and started with Genesis and that's as far as you got? Or maybe you've read as far as Chronicles and been finished off there. One time I saw a *Reader's Digest* article that was titled, "We're Up to Chronicles." *That* was worth putting in the *Reader's Digest.* The devil will do anything he can to keep us from learning about the love of God. It is possible to know about everything in the Bible *except* the love of God. It is possible to understand about history and prophecy and beasts and symbols and all that, and still to have missed the love of God.

Then there are the pseudo-intellectuals who like to talk about religion but spend very little time with the Word and communicating with God. They spend a great deal of time discussing and dissecting and analyzing God and religion. They want to forget God in a way that will pass as remembering Him. They discuss what will happen to flowers that people pick in heaven or whether angels' wings have feathers—or they take more sophisticated side trips. But they never mention the name of Jesus, and the devil sits back and laughs.

Some people substitute behavioral changes for a personal relationship with God. If they succeed in changing their behavior, they think they've found Him. Some depend on other people, and their spiritual life varies from high to low according to what kind of people they're around. Some become preoccupied with a psychological approach that doesn't have God as the center. They analyze themselves and forget Christ. Some people escape a relationship with God by being just too busy to take time for Him. But all the time God is following, staying close, helping when we don't know it, guiding when we don't intend it, ever trying to bring us to a true knowledge of Himself, whom to know is life eternal.

STEP 3: ADMIT YOU ARE A SINNER

The knowledge of the love of God as revealed in the plan of salvation will lead to the third step in coming to Christ, *conviction of sin.*

The behaviorist defines sin in terms of transgression of the law. It's true—that is the only legal, forensic definition of sin in the Bible (1 John 3:4). But the Bible has some experiential definitions of sin that go deeper than that. One of the best is in Romans 14:23, "Whatsoever is not of faith is sin." Whatever we do, if we don't do it through faith in Christ, is sin.

Another definition involves two terms: *sin,* singular, and *sins,* plural. *Sin* is living a life without Christ. *Sins* are transgressions of the law. Living a life apart from Christ—*sin*—is the cause of our doing wrong things—*sins.* King James's Bible scholars translated 1 John 3:4 in an interesting way: "Whosoever committeth sin [whoever lives a life apart from Christ] transgresseth *also* the law" (emphasis added).

When did Eve sin? When she ate the fruit? She sinned when she distrusted what God had told her. Eating the fruit was simply the natural result of that. If I am doing wrong things, sinful things, my real problem is that I am living a life apart from Christ. Either that or I haven't known Him long enough yet to grow to victory. Jesus Himself allowed for growth.

So when we talk about conviction, we are talking about the realization that we are sinners *regardless of what we have done. Regardless of how good or bad we have been.* We were born sinners—born sinful by nature. "All unrighteousness is sin" (1 John 5:17). "There is none righteous" (Romans 3:10). So there is nobody righteous, we are all unrighteous, and all unrighteousness is sin. But don't ever feel that we are held responsible for being born in a world of sin. Jesus knows where we were born, and the only thing we are responsible for is what we do with His plan of salvation.

When we face ourselves in the presence of Jesus, we become convicted that we are sinners—*not because of what we have done but because of what we are.* Through this conviction, we realize our need of Him.

STEP 4: REALIZE YOU ARE HELPLESS

When we have been convicted that we are sinners, whether or not we have ever done anything wrong, and when we have repented of our sinfulness, the next step in coming to Christ is to admit that we are helpless to change our lives. We don't change our lives in order to come to Christ. We come to Christ, and *He* changes our lives. Many people say, "Well, when I can fix up my life so that it is good enough, then I will come to Christ." They should stop wasting their time and energy. They're taking on a hopeless task. All of us are helpless.

The whole message of salvation through faith in Christ alone can be summed up in two verses. The first, John 15:5, says, "Without me ye can do nothing." How much is nothing? *Nothing*—that's how much it is.

The second verse is Philippians 4:13, "I can do all things through Christ." How many things? *All things!*

So, it's just that simple. The youngest boy and girl can understand it. Without Him, I can do nothing. With Him, I can do everything. So, the only possible thing I can do is to get with Christ. That's all I can do to be saved.

"But," you say, "some people are helpless and some aren't. What about the strong people who are doing pretty well? Are they really helpless?"

Yes, they are! The strong people can control the externals. But the problem is deeper than the externals. "Education, culture, the exercise of the will, human effort, all have their proper sphere, but *here* they are powerless."[2] "Our *hearts* are evil, and we cannot change them."[3] Neither the strong nor the weak can change their inward life. Both must admit their helplessness and come to Christ just as they are.

STEP 5: SURRENDER YOURSELF TO CHRIST

The term *surrender* is grossly misunderstood by multitudes of Christians. If people's idea of Christianity is based upon behavior, then their primary focus will be on the Ten Commandments and trying hard to obey them. If the people are strong, they will "succeed." If they are weak, they will fail. The behaviorist philosophy never brings those who follow it to the point of surrender. Behaviorists who are strong and apparently successful don't realize they are helpless. They don't think they need to surrender—they're "doing all right." Behaviorists who are weak don't surrender either. They say, "I can't do it; I give up," and quit trying to obey and go away from God when they've reached the very point—if they only knew it—where they are closer to God than they may ever be again.

Behaviorists think that surrender is giving up certain *things* in their life—giving up their sins, giving up their problems and weaknesses. So they say, "I stand before God and this audience, and I promise that from now on, I won't smoke, drink, or dance anymore." If they are strong, they never do them again—and they become so-called good church members. If surrender has primarily to do with giving up *things,* the strong succeed and the weak fail.

I've heard a lot of different gimmicks for giving up sins, giving up things. I've even heard of people writing their sins on pieces of paper and passing them to the aisle, where they are all collected and brought to the front of the church. Someone lights a match at a little altar there and burns the "sins" up. Wonderful! The sins are "gone" now. They're "all burned up." But that's a psychological gimmick, and when the weak people who wrote their sins down on pieces of paper in order to burn them up go home, they discover they still have them.

Some people have tried every gimmick in the book until finally they've said, "I guess some people are born to be fuel for the fires of hell, and I must be one of them." They begin to believe in predestination. But notice what Paul wrote to the Romans:

> What shall we say then? That the Gentiles, which followed
> not after righteousness, have attained to righteousness, even
> the righteousness which is of faith. But Israel, which followed
> after the law of righteousness, hath not attained to the law of
> righteousness. Wherefore? [In other words, why?] Because

they sought it not by faith, but as it were by the works of the law. [They were behaviorists.] For they stumbled at that stumblingstone; as it is written, Behold, I lay in Sion a stumblingstone and rock of offence: and whosoever believeth on him shall not be ashamed. . . . For I bear them record that they have a zeal of God, but not according to knowledge. For they being ignorant of God's righteousness, and going about to establish their own righteousness, have not submitted themselves unto the righteousness of God (Romans 9:30–10:3).

Remember this: An apple tree bears apples because it *is* an apple tree, never in order *to be* one. If you want to grow apples, the best thing for you to do is to get an apple tree. An apple tree doesn't have to try hard to produce apples; it's natural for an apple tree to produce apples. Here's a paraphrase of that scripture I quoted above:

What shall we say then? That the Gentiles who weren't trying to produce apples have produced apples, even the apples that come from the apple tree. But the Israelites, who were trying to produce apples, have not produced apples. Why? Because they didn't try to become apple trees but instead tried to produce apples by their own efforts. For they, being ignorant of God's way of producing fruit, and going about to produce their own apples, have not submitted themselves unto becoming apple trees. For Christ is the end of trying to produce apples apart from the apple tree to everyone who will become an apple tree. (That's Venden's Revised Standard Version!)

Christians do right because they *are* Christians, never in order *to be* Christians. Giving up on our own ability to produce the fruits of righteousness—admitting that we can't do it—is the beginning of the Christian life.

Surrender is not giving up *things*. Surrender is giving up the idea that we can do anything at all about the things that interfere with living a Christian life—anything except one: we can come to Christ just as we are. We must surrender *ourselves* to Him.

STEP 6: RECEIVE THE GIFT OF REPENTANCE

Jesus loves to have us come to Him just as we are. Repentance is not our work, not a condition for acceptance with Him. We are told that this is "a point on which many may err, and hence they fail of receiving the help that Christ desires to give them. They think that they cannot come to Christ unless they first repent."[4] But repentance is a gift. We receive this gift when we come to Christ.

In Revelation 3:19, the Laodicean church is admonished to be zealous and repent. For those of us living during the time in the earth's history when we are at least potential Laodiceans, it is of utmost importance that we understand the nature of true repentance. It is not a matter of working hard to make ourselves feel sorry. Acts 5:31 tells us that God exalted Jesus "to be a Prince and a Saviour, for to *give* repentance to Israel, and forgiveness of sins" (emphasis added). "Repentance is no less the gift of God than are pardon and justification, and it cannot be experienced except as it is given to the soul by Christ."[5] So if you want repentance for today, you can go to your knees and ask God for it, because it is a gift and He delights to give good gifts to His children. Notice 2 Corinthians 7:10, "Godly sorrow worketh repentance to salvation not to be repented of: but the sorrow of the world worketh death." Where do we get godly sorrow? From God! We don't work it up ourselves.

We need to understand what it is that Laodiceans need to repent of. It is *not* primarily immorality. Laodiceans are quite moral. Laodiceans are known for their external goodness. But in spite of that, the Savior is standing on the outside, knocking, seeking admission. What Laodiceans need to repent of is their *morality*—their many good works *apart from Jesus.*

We need to repent of living lives centered and focused on anything other than Christ. Is Jesus the central focus of your home, your life, and your relationships? Is He the theme of your thoughts, your conversations? Or do you need to come to Him for repentance for having kept Him knocking on the outside of your heart?

When my brother and I were in college, we were roommates. This was rather unexpected because we had spent much of our time up until then fighting with each other. Our parents used to worry that we would never live to grow up. But we found out when we got to college that we were very close. Psychologists tell us that it is common for people to fight with those they love—that if they didn't love them, they wouldn't waste their time fighting with them! Maybe that was the underlying cause of all our arguments. But when we were room-mates, we got along very well.

We used to clean the room every Friday to prepare for the Sabbath. One week, though, I was trying to finish a term paper the Friday before the deadline. My brother came in while I was typing away. "Quick! Hurry!" he said. "We've got to do the room!"

I said, "You do it. I can't. I'm too busy." And we began to teeter on the edge of the combat precipice again.

But then my brother relaxed and said, "That's all right. That's perfectly all right. I understand. You must be under terrible pressure. It must be mighty hard for you. I'll clean the room. I'm happy to clean the room. I'll do it all by myself. You go ahead and work on your paper."

He broke my heart! I put down my paper, and I helped clean the room.

We used that approach on each other many times after that. We used it only in fun, but it was a simple illustration of the fact that when someone doesn't act against you but rather gives evidence of loving acceptance, he or she wins you over—right? The "goodness" of my brother led me to help clean the room.

In Romans 2:4, the Bible says it is the goodness of God that leads us to repentance. The goodness of God is real. It isn't faked. It's the only kind of real goodness there is.

Are you seeking for genuine repentance? As you come to Christ, study His life, contemplate His character and mission, and understand His great love and acceptance for you, you will be brought to repentance.

A CONTINUING EXPERIENCE

Conversion is more than saying Yes to God one time. When people wake up the week after the week before and discover that they still have some of the same problems, weaknesses, and fears, they're tempted to think it must not have really happened after all. They don't realize that often the devil works harder when he sees someone come to Christ than he ever did before. Things may go worse after conversion than they did before. There may be more trials, more temptations, and more defeats than before the decision was made. Have you seen it happen? The devil tries everything he knows to get us to give up and forget about God.

A great many people think they must not have really come to Christ because their surrender didn't last. That's one of the big dilemmas in the Christian world today. There are hundreds of people who have sincerely come to Jesus with a great sense of need and have later become disenchanted when the conversion seemed to fade away. It is possible for us to have genuinely accepted Christ and given up on self during a Week of Prayer last year or on the sawdust trail forty years ago but to have the commitment die because we've done nothing about it since.

If conversion isn't immediate victory, peace, and freedom from temptation and trial, what is it? Here's a definition of conversion that is based on two chapters in *The Desire of Ages,* "Nicodemus" and "At Jacob's Well": conversion is a supernatural work of the Holy Spirit upon the human heart that produces a change of attitude toward God and creates a new capacity for knowing God. In order to grow in the Christian life, we must renew our conversion every day.

However, conversion is God's work, never ours. When we are born again, instead of being against God, we're on His side. And conversion brings a relish for spiritual things that were foolishness to us while we were at enmity with God. Conversion isn't the end point of spiritual life any more than physical birth is the end point of physical life. It is only the equipment you need to start living the spiritual life. It is only the beginning.

THE DEVIL'S RESPONSE

When a person first begins to understand that God offers a life of freedom, peace, and fulfillment through righteousness by faith in Jesus, the devil becomes nervous. He has worked for as long as possible to keep everyone from having any interest in God whatever. He doesn't want anybody to come to Jesus and find rest. The further away we stay, the better he likes it. But if he fails to keep us from being drawn to Jesus, fails to keep us from searching into the things of God, he begins to use other tactics.

The first of these is to try to get us to work on righteousness. We can spend years of futile effort working hard on the externals, trying to make ourselves good enough to be accepted by God. Finally, the realization comes that righteousness is by faith in Jesus alone. We learn that external goodness is insufficient. We see that our hearts are evil and we cannot change them, even if we are successful in improving our behavior.

At this point, the devil comes in with another clever sidetrack. He tries to get us to work on our faith. He brings in all his arguments in favor of positive thinking and urges us to concentrate on making ourselves believe. He tries to get us more interested in claiming promises than in the One who made the promises. When we pray primarily for answers and we don't get the answers we expect, he can then destroy our faith in God while we profess to be exercising it.

When we realize that we can't develop either righteousness *or* faith by our own efforts, the devil makes his final attempt to keep us from coming to Christ. "*Now* you've got it right," he says. "What you need to do is to give up. You must try hard to give up."

Many of us have tried time and time again to make ourselves surrender—until we heard the good news that surrender is also a gift, as surely as righteousness and faith are gifts. "No man can empty himself of self. We can only consent for Christ to accomplish the work."[6]

Every gift that God has to give us, righteousness, peace, faith, victory, eternal life, and even surrender, is available in only one way—by coming into relationship with the Giver through personal communication with Him.

The preceding chapter is based on material from Morris Venden's book Faith That Works *(Hagerstown, Md.: Review and Herald®, 1980). Used by permission.*

1. Ellen G. White, *Selected Messages* (Washington, D.C.: Review and Herald®, 1958), 1:323.

2. Ellen G. White, *Steps to Christ* (Mountain View, Calif.: Pacific Press®, 1956), 18; emphasis added.

3. Ibid.; emphasis added.

4. White, *Steps to Christ*, 26.

5. White, *Selected Messages,* 1:391.

6. Ellen G. White, *Christ's Object Lessons* (Washington, D.C.: Review and Herald®, 1941), 159.

Chapter 8

JESUS

CHARLES T. EVERSON

In earlier chapters, we have noted the part that lifting Jesus up plays in the process of conversion. Jesus said that when He is lifted up, He will draw all people to Himself (John 12:32). In this chapter, we will focus on Jesus through a sermon preached by Charles T. Everson, one of the greatest evangelists of the twentieth century. This sermon is still being used, in print form, to bring sinners to Christ. God used Everson to bring H. M. S. Richards Sr. into the work of evangelism and thus, through the Voice of Prophecy *radio program, to bring Christ to the millions.*

All power in heaven and earth centers in the person of Jesus. Everything that people need in this world and in the world to come is found in Him. Without Him, no one can hope to succeed, but with Him, failure is impossible. No human mind has ever been able to comprehend the height, the depth, the length, and the breadth of the eternal realities that reside in Jesus, for He contains all the fullness of the Godhead bodily (Colossians 2:9).

It is clear that in order for Jesus to be so mighty, He must be more than a mere man. Many centuries before He came, it was foretold of Him in Isaiah 9:6, "Unto us a child is born, unto us a son is given: and the government shall be upon his shoulder: and his name shall be called Wonderful, Counsellor, The mighty God, The everlasting Father, The Prince of Peace."

Isaiah, looking down over more than seven centuries of time, saw the Prince of Peace born into this world. Speaking under the inspiration of the Spirit, the prophet boldly affirmed that this Child who was to be born is "the mighty God." No one could possibly have fulfilled the predictions made in this prophecy unless he was born as a child and at the same time was the mighty God.

There are very few in the present generation who refuse to believe that Christ was a real historical character—that He was born into the world and lived His life among humanity. There are a considerable number of people, however, who will not admit that Jesus Christ is God. The testimony of Bible prophecy to the deity of Jesus Christ is conclusive.

It is said concerning the apostle Paul, who was actually a contemporary of the Lord Jesus Christ, that he had the philosophical mind of a Plato and the literary genius of a Shakespeare. Being a contemporary of Jesus, Paul did not investigate the claims of Jesus when centuries had passed and the real person of Christ might have been lost in the midst of mythology and hero worship. He scrutinized those claims when Christianity was in its infancy, when the generation in which Jesus lived was still alive. To the mind of the apostle Paul, one of the most conclusive reasons for believing Jesus Christ to be the Divine Son of God was the fact that He rose from the dead. In Romans 1:1–4, he wrote of "the gospel of God . . . concerning His Son Jesus Christ our Lord, which was made of the seed of David according to the flesh; and declared to be the Son of God with power, according to the spirit of holiness, by the resurrection from the dead."

Paul tells us here that Christ is of the seed of David according to the flesh, but on the divine side of His nature, He is declared to be the Son of God by His resurrection from the dead. The resurrection of Christ must not be left in doubt down through the ages, for on it rests the most potent argument of all in favor of the divinity of Christ. If there is nothing left of the mighty Man of Nazareth except a handful of dust in an old Syrian tomb, to what hope of a future life can we look forward?

So God raised up Paul with his brilliant mind that he might investigate the claims of the resurrection of Christ while the people were still alive who said they actually saw Him after He rose from the dead. He tells us that after the Resurrection, Jesus was seen by more than five hundred persons at once. The greater part of this number were still alive when Paul had attained the prominence of an apostle in the early church (1 Corinthians 15:6). He was able to obtain their personal testimony to the certainty of the Resurrection. These were men and women outside the circle of the apostles.

It would be difficult indeed to find any event in history to which the unanimous testimony of five hundred persons could be obtained. Yet this is the testimony given concerning the resurrection of Jesus Christ, which makes it the most accredited and certain historical event of all time. No wonder Talleyrand, the secretary of state under Napoleon Bonaparte, said that there is no event in all history the certainty of which is so fully established as the resurrection of Christ.

Of course, the apostles themselves affirmed that they saw Him and talked with Him after He rose from the dead, so they had not a shadow of doubt regarding His resurrection. May we again quote the statement of Paul? "Declared to be the Son of God with power . . . by the resurrection from the dead." Surely Jesus is the eternal Son of God.

Paul saw that Jesus was like a great mountain peak that pushed its snowcapped summit into the clouds, and all other people were but like the swamps at its base. One eminent authority has said concerning the apostle Paul that he was the greatest man who ever lived. And yet this great man said that he himself was but refuse in comparison to Jesus. When we see how far Jesus Christ towers above Paul, considered the greatest and best of human beings, it is clear that Jesus must be more than human.

If Jesus were not more than a man, it would be impossible to explain the influence of His life. Everything about Him points to the fact that He is not a mere man but is actually God. He was born in a stable and cradled in a manger, yet around that manger and that precious Babe the whole world gathers at least once a year and stops and listens anew to the angels' song of peace on earth and goodwill to men, and all the world becomes tender and is drawn closer together.

Other babes have been born during the centuries, but none of them have gripped the heart of the world as has this One.

Out of the dimly lighted stable of Bethlehem comes a light that makes the hearts of people glow with a warmth that inspires them to the loftiest acts of which they are capable. The poor and the hungry are fed, the homeless are given shelter, and the naked are clothed. The hardfisted and selfish suddenly wake up and become unselfish, sending good cheer into the desolate homes of the unfortunate. Who can explain the mighty hold that Jesus has on the hearts of men and women except by admitting that Jesus Christ is more than human?

Jesus was no visionary who sat and dreamed and philosophized as the days came and went. He was a hard-working artisan who applied Himself to the carpenter's trade in the village of Nazareth, in Galilee. Until He was thirty years old, He worked early and late at the carpenter's bench.

At an age that had sunk to the lowest ebb of iniquity and sin, Nazareth was an outstanding example of moral depravity. Its reputation for wickedness was so great that it had become proverbial. The saying was current in Christ's day, "Can there any good thing come out of Nazareth?" The product of this town was expected to be nothing but vile and sinful.

In this town Jesus spent the greater part of His life, living there nearly thirty of the thirty-three and a half years of His sojourn on earth. It was not an environment that was calculated to grow a rare and choice plant. Yet amid those vile surroundings grew the Lily of the valley that has sent forth its fragrance of purity to lift the whole world to a higher and loftier plane. This was possible because He did not depend for His spiritual sustenance upon the soil of Nazareth but drew His strength from the very throne of heaven.

YEARS IN OBSCURITY

Very little is known of the life of Jesus Christ during His sojourn in Nazareth. Practically all we know is that He worked as a humble carpenter there until He was thirty years of age. He died at the age of thirty-three and a half. Only three and one-half years of His life were lived outside the obscurity of the little carpenter's shop of Nazareth. During that brief time, He wandered about on the dusty roads of a small country, Palestine, which was at that time a vassal of Rome. Jesus did not share in the educational advantages of His time. He never wrote a book, never traveled, never had a job or a public office. He never was seated upon a royal throne in this world, never was a governor—not even a mayor of a town or even a constable of a small village; and He died as a criminal. Everybody, apparently, was glad when He passed away, except a few fishermen and some humble women.

Abraham Lincoln was president of a great nation and was sincerely mourned by millions, but when Jesus died, He was execrated by His nation and mourned by but a few unlearned followers. He died upon a cross—an ignominious death reserved for the slave and the alien. And yet His name eclipses all others, and He is the outstanding Figure of the centuries.

The cross was the gallows of His day—the electric chair of His age. It was the cruelest instrument of torture ever invented. Men were nailed upon it and hung there unsheltered from the biting cold or the scorching heat until they died of exhaustion or of heartbreaking suffering. We are told by historians that some lived for a week hanging upon the cross, until the birds came and plucked out their eyes while they were still alive.

The body of the Lord Jesus touched the cruel cross and immediately transformed it into the glory of the world. We have our red crosses, our white crosses, our green crosses, with all their crossed pieces like friendly arms reaching out to heal and uplift and bless the world. What woman would think of wearing a representation of the electric chair as an ornament about her neck, or what man would suspend a model of a gallows as a watch charm from his pocket? Yet today we find the once cruel instrument of torture, the cross, gladly worn by men and women as the symbol of all that is good and noble and inspiring and holy. What a mighty Person this Man Jesus must be, whose one touch can change an instrument of cruelty, suffering, and shame into the world's greatest symbol of peace and goodwill.

Mary, the mother of the Lord Jesus, was a woman of modest circumstances brought up among the rugged hills of old Galilee. Her life was one of hardship and poverty. At the critical moment of her life, when every woman especially needs a friend, she was obliged to find her way into a dimly lighted stable at the time of the birth of her first-born Son, Jesus. And yet this humble girl of Galilee has become the most honored and revered woman in all history. Her name, *Mary*, has become a household word in nearly every nation of the world. The only reason why such signal honor has been bestowed upon her is that she is the mother of Jesus Christ. The name of Jesus lifts the simple girl out of the commonplace into the sublime. What a mighty name is this name of Jesus!

Every time you write the number of the year on your letter, or make an entry into your ledger, or look for the date on your newspaper or magazine, you are reminded that Jesus was born so many years ago. This year is numbered as it is because Jesus was born into the world. Other great men have lived since His day, but He remains supreme through the ages. It is not so many years after Julius Caesar, or Shakespeare, or Napoleon, or Washington, or Abraham Lincoln, but it is so many years after Jesus Christ.

The first thing that meets you when you enter the classroom is that everything in history is dated before and after Jesus Christ. He is the Number One of history. From this Number One, Jesus Christ, you count all the events of all time. Like a great mountain peak pushing its snowcapped head into the clouds, He stands supreme, and all history slopes down from Him. He splits the centuries in two, and all history revolves about His name.

Who can explain this without admitting that Jesus Christ is more than mere man? His public career lasted only three and a half years, but from that three and a half years of short, fleeting ministry, His life sent forth a power that has lifted empires off their hinges, turned the centuries out of their course, and colored the stream of time with His blood. Think back over three and one-half years of your own life, and see how quickly they have passed, and how little impression you have made even on your immediate surroundings, to say nothing of the world at large. Jesus wandered around three and one-half years without office or position in any land, with a few humble followers, and yet today He is the dominant Figure of history. So great an effect must have a corresponding cause.

William E. Lecky, the noted Irish historian, in his *Essays on Religion,* has summed up the life of Christ in the following language:

> It was reserved for Christianity to present to the world an ideal character, which, through all the changes of eighteen centuries, has inspired the hearts of men with an impassioned love, and has shown itself capable of acting on all ages, nations, temperaments, and conditions; has not only been the highest patron of virtue, but the highest incentive to its practice, and has exerted so deep an influence that it may be truly said that the simple record of those short years of active life has done more to regenerate and to soften mankind than all the disquisitions of philosophers and all the exhortations of moralists.[1]

THE UNIVERSAL CHRIST

Christ was born of Jewish stock and lived His entire life among the Jews; yet no one thinks of Him as a Jew. The prejudice that is sometimes held against that race is certainly absent when men think of Christ. He is loved everywhere, and all nations call Him their own. When the Frenchman paints Him, He looks like a Frenchman. When the Italian depicts Him upon the canvas, He is an Italian; the German always makes Him look like a German in his pictures; and the American paints Him so that He looks like an American. He rises above all national lines and all national borders, and is the universal Christ, loved and worshiped in every nation. His name is sung and prayed in more than eight hundred languages in the world today.

He is the Supreme Figure of the ages, and is growing more mighty every day. Kings, potentates, and crowns are falling rapidly. Great names, one after the other, flicker and go out and are soon forgotten, but the name of Jesus is ever increasing in might and glory. It is the one name that goes steadily marching on. How can you account for such a tremendous effect without admitting a corresponding cause?

What great name but the name of Jesus helps people die in peace? Millions of persons have passed into the valley of the shadow of death with the name of Jesus on their parched lips, and for them the valley has been transformed with light and glory, and the shadows have fled away as the Sun of Righteousness has lighted up their last moments with resplendent colors. Surely Jesus must be divine.

Napoleon Bonaparte gives us this testimony:

> Across a chasm of eighteen hundred years Jesus Christ makes a demand which is, beyond all others, difficult to satisfy. He asks that for which a philosopher may seek in vain at the hands of his friends, or a father of his children, or a bride of her husband, or a man of his brother. He asks for the human heart; He will have it entirely to Himself. He demands it unconditionally, and forthwith His demand is granted. Wonderful! In defiance of time and space, the soul of man, with all its powers and faculties, becomes an annexation to the empire of Christ. All who sincerely believe in Him experience that remarkable, supernatural love toward Him. This phenomenon is unaccountable. It is beyond the scope of man's creative power. Time, the great destroyer, is powerless to extinguish this sacred flame. Time can neither exhaust its strength nor put a limit to its reign. This is what strikes me most. I have often thought of it. This is what to me proves quite convincingly the divinity of Jesus Christ.

Shortly before Jesus Christ went to His death upon the cross, He made a wonderful pronouncement. We read in Matthew 24:14, "This gospel of the kingdom shall be preached in all the world for a witness unto all nations; and then shall the end come."

Jesus Christ was standing alone, looking, as it were, at the open tomb. His nation had given Him up. At Rome, the capital of the world, He was unknown. His few followers would soon leave Him and flee. Yet when He stood at what would seem to be the end of the road, His eyes were not dimmed with the tears of disappointment, for He looked with the eyes of God upon the future generations, and He said, "There is coming a day in which My name and My gospel will be known around the world."

At the time He made this pronouncement, there was not a chance in the world, according to human probabilities, that what He predicted could happen; but it has come true nevertheless. Today, men and women are telling the story of Jesus throughout Africa. In China they are singing the praises of the Christ of God. Their hearts are glowing with the thought of the gospel of Jesus in the islands of the sea. In fact, every country in the world is hearing the name of Jesus in song and in scriptural language.

At a time when the whole world was lying in the inky blackness of heathenism and the only nation that really believed in God was hostile to Him and gave Him up to be crucified, how did Jesus Christ know that there would come a day when His praises and His gospel would be sounded to the end of the earth? He knew it because Jesus Christ is God, and God knows the end from the beginning. Men do not know the future. If we knew what the future held in store for us, how different would be our plans! But God alone is able to foretell and unveil future events.

There is one other beautiful thing about this pronouncement. Jesus tells us that when His name is sounded around the world and the gospel is preached in every nation, then will the end come—the end of the reign of sin and sorrow and heartbreak and trouble. As we stand looking over the world and see this marvelous prediction so fully and wonderfully fulfilling, we may know that we are nearing the dawn of that better day when sin will be no more. We are approaching that time when the nations of the world shall become the kingdoms of our Lord and of His Christ, and He shall reign forever and ever.

How wonderful to live in a country of which Jesus Christ, the Man of Calvary, the One who gave His life for us, is King. What a wonderful Ruler He will make in that country of the blessed!

"What value is it to us," you say, "to know that Jesus Christ is God?"

Well, dear friends, Jesus Christ is God, and God cannot lie. So the story He tells us in the Scriptures must be true. There *is* a home over there where the changes never come. There *is* a land that is fairer than day. There *is* a country where people can run and not be weary, and walk and never be faint. This life is altogether too short even for the person who lives to a ripe old age. How comforting it is to know that there is a place prepared for those who are willing to live for and to love this dear Jesus—a place where their fondest ambitions will be realized and where men and women will live with perfect minds in perfect bodies in a perfect world forever.

PRECIOUS NAME!

Jesus! How wonderful and precious is the name! He is the Prince of Peace, the mighty God, and the coming King. When we think of Him who was born in a stable and died upon a cross; who divides the centuries in two, and about whose name all history revolves; who lifted empires off their hinges, turning the stream of time out of its course; and who at the same time binds up the brokenhearted and speaks peace to the troubled breast; when we think of the millions who have died with the name of Jesus on their parched lips, and of how the shadows of death have burst into the glorious colors of the setting sun at the thought of Him, may we not exclaim:

"All hail the power of Jesus' name,
　　Let angels prostrate fall;

Bring forth the royal diadem,
   And crown Him Lord of all."

All the glories that gather round that name sublime are wonderful to behold, but they will be of no value to you, dear friend, unless Jesus makes a triumphant entry into your heart. You must do something definite about the acceptance of Christ as your personal Savior if His life is to benefit you.

Perhaps you are saying within your heart, "I admit that I am not what might be called a real Christian, but I believe I have as good a chance for heaven as some people I know who profess to belong to Christ."

Let me give you an illustration that I hope will make this matter of the need of accepting Christ still clearer. In Rome, Italy, some years ago, there entered the office of the American embassy a man who appeared to be in great distress. When he finally secured an audience with the ambassador, he stated his case, a very serious one, and then implored the ambassador for help. The ambassador immediately asked the man, "Are you a citizen of the United States?"

The man replied, "I have lived in the United States for twenty-five years. I have reared my family there. I have always paid my taxes and contributed to all worthy enterprises."

"But," interrupted the ambassador, "are you a citizen of the United States?"

The man answered slowly, "No, I have never taken out citizenship papers; but I believe I have done my duty toward the government just as fully as those who have taken out their citizenship papers."

The ambassador replied, "I am sorry for you, but I cannot help you because you are not a citizen of my country."

Some years later, a man entered the same embassy and talked to the same ambassador. The man was trembling with fear and emotion, for his case was desperate. He spoke in broken English, but he stated his case to the ambassador with sufficient clearness to make him understand his situation. The ambassador directed the same question to this man that he had asked the other man some years before: "Are you a citizen of the United States?"

In a faltering manner, the anxious man told the ambassador that some years before, he had taken out his first papers, and just before he sailed for Italy, he had received his last papers, and so he was a full-fledged citizen of the United States.

The ambassador exclaimed, "You are a citizen of my country. I extend to you the full power of the United States for your protection, and one hundred thirty million American citizens are behind you to see that you get your rights."

No foreigner can become a citizen of a country without making a positive, definite decision to take out his citizenship papers. Everyone is a foreigner by nature with respect to the kingdom of heaven. But we may become "fellowcitizens with the saints," as Paul expressed it in Ephesians 2:19. So may I ask you the question, "Have you taken out citizenship papers that entitle you to a place in the kingdom of heaven?" It is not a question of how near you think you come to doing as well as your neighbors who are Christians. The question is, Have you taken out your citizenship papers? Is Christ the King of your heart now?

You say, "I do not know how to take out citizenship papers for heaven."

If you are willing to acknowledge Christ as your personal Savior, to follow Him all the way, He will accept you as a citizen of His kingdom, and you will become right now a citizen of the kingdom of grace. You cannot do His will without His help, so it is useless to talk about being saved at last unless He has entered your heart and taken up His abode there. Our part of the transaction is to be willing to do God's will. Christ's part is to furnish the power to do the thing you will to do.

We have the case of a palsied man mentioned in Luke 5:18—a helpless, bedridden victim. Jesus told him to arise and take up his bed and go to his house. No doubt this palsied man had tried many times to rise but had found that he was absolutely helpless. But when Jesus told him to arise, he made the effort, and immediately Christ furnished the power, and he was able to rise. So with us. If we are willing to make the effort, taking Christ at His word, He will furnish the power to do God's will.

Will you not bow your head and accept Him, and invite Him to take charge of your life? He will come in and live His life within you, and at last He will present you faultless before the throne (Jude 24). May you not delay. May you make the decision in favor of Christ and eternity right now. Then a peace that floweth like a river will be yours for time and eternity.

This chapter was taken from Charles T. Everson's book Jesus *(Hagerstown, Md.: Review and Herald®, 1984). Used by permission.*

---

1. William E. Lecky, *Essays on Religion*, 253.

Chapter 9

INTERCESSORY PRAYER

MORRIS VENDEN

In this chapter, we will find that although we will never be responsible for the destiny of others, we can have a part in their conversion. The chapter explains biblically and simply how this can be. Will someone be lost if we don't share and tell? Yes, we will be lost—not someone else. God has given us the wonderful opportunity of leading others to salvation. It is a great privilege to work together with Him in this way.

One day a woman went to visit the pastor of her church. She said, "I am concerned for my husband. He has never been converted. Would you please pray for him?"

The pastor replied, "I will pray for your husband for one hour every day, if you will pray for your husband for one hour every day."

After considering the matter briefly, the woman said, "Never mind," and she left the office.

What's your reaction to this woman? Did you think, *Well, that pastor sure knew how to smoke her out of the woods. Obviously, she wasn't that concerned about her husband after all?* Or did you think, *That woman was just being honest, admitting that she wouldn't be able to keep up her end of the bargain?*

What would you do if someone made a similar offer to you? Some of us would have agreed to the arrangement and then would have struggled through ten or fifteen minutes the first day, and five minutes the second day, and after that have hoped that the pastor would follow through even though we didn't! Would you be able to pray faithfully for your friend or relative for one hour every day? Have you ever prayed for an entire hour for just one person? Could you do it again the next day—and the day after that, and the day after that?

In a church that I pastored several years ago, we decided to have, during our Wednesday night meetings, a series on the subject of prayer. It didn't take long for the one key question to arise, What difference does prayer make? If you pray for someone, and that person knows you are praying for him, perhaps that would have some psychological benefit. But what if you pray for someone who doesn't know you are praying for him? Does that help? How could it? Why would it? After all, is it fair for God to bless this person here, who has someone praying for him, and to withhold a blessing from that person over there just because she doesn't have anyone praying for her?

After twisting our brains all out of shape for a while, someone finally suggested, "Why don't we try it and find out? Let's choose an impossible case and pray for that person both in the group on Wednesday nights and privately in our homes. Let's see what happens."

I had visited an "impossible case" that very day. There was a family in the community who had been members of the church years before. In fact, they had even been to the mission field. But someone had done them wrong, and they felt disillusioned, bitter, and angry. They hated the church. They hated preachers. As I left their home that afternoon, they had shouted, "And don't pray for us!" However, they had no control over that!

So I mentioned the names of these people to the congregation. Everyone nodded in agreement. The family was well-known in the community. It was truly an impossible case. We decided to make that family our test case. We would pray for them specifically in our private prayers at home all through the week.

That first week their house burned down! The news came out in the local paper. When we gathered for prayer meeting the following

Wednesday, I asked my congregation, "What are you people praying for, anyway?"

We continued praying. The second week, the newspaper reported that a valuable piece of equipment that this family used in their business had been stolen. And so it went. One thing after another went wrong for them. We just kept on praying and watching.

The last Sabbath of that month, the entire family walked into church. Heads turned—and then quickly turned back again—and word flew from one person to another, "They're here!" After church, one by one the people came to me and said, "We ought to do more praying!"

WHY DOES PRAYER MAKE A DIFFERENCE?

The Lord is the Judge—the Righteous Judge of the universe. It's an analogy that is found often in Scripture. Paul said, "There is laid up for me a crown of righteousness, which the Lord, the righteous judge, shall give me at that day: and not to me only, but unto all them also that love his appearing" (2 Timothy 4:8). Another familiar verse is 1 John 2:1, "My little children, these things write I unto you, that ye sin not. And if any man sin, we have an advocate with the Father, Jesus Christ the righteous."

What is an advocate? These are some of the other words that mean the same thing: *lawyer, attorney, intercessor, mediator.* Isaiah 53:12 points to Jesus as Intercessor for transgressors. Romans 8:34 says that Christ is at the right hand of God making intercession for us. Hebrews 7:25 says that Jesus "ever liveth to make intercession for" us. First Timothy 2:5, 6 speaks of Jesus as the Mediator between God and man. These words describe the roles of Jesus and the Father in Their relationship to us.

That is good Bible evidence as to why God can do things when we pray that He can't do when we don't pray. Mediators, intercessors, and appeals-court judges would be overstepping their bounds if they took on cases that had not been appealed to them. Defense attorneys watch like hawks for any opportunity to declare a mistrial. If judges were to take on cases that hadn't been appealed to them, you can be sure the defense attorneys would make the most of it!

So it is with God the Father and Jesus and even the Holy Spirit, who intercedes for us with "groanings which cannot be uttered" (Romans 8:26). Although They are anxious to work in our behalf, there are certain limitations. When we pray for ourselves or for others and appeal a case to Them, They are free to work in a way that otherwise They could not. This is one of the reasons, in terms of the great controversy, why prayer makes a difference. But the next thing we need to understand is what kind of difference prayer *can* make—and what kind of difference prayer *cannot* make.

Let's try another parable! Let's say that one day you are walking from San Francisco to Pacific Union College (PUC)—the "Promised Land"! I come driving along in my car, pull over beside you, and ask, "Where are you going?"

"I'm going to Pacific Union College—the Promised Land," you say.

"That's where I'm going," I reply. "Get in, and I'll take you there."

Now you will arrive at PUC a lot faster. You will get fewer blisters along the way and have an easier trip. But you *were* going to get there anyway.

Now let's reverse the picture. One day, you are walking from San Francisco to Las Vegas—the other place! I come driving along in my car, pull over beside you, and ask, "Where are you going?"

You say, "I'm going to Las Vegas—the other place!"

"That's where I'm going too," I say. "Get in, and I'll take you there."

Now you will arrive at Las Vegas a lot faster. You will get fewer blisters along the way—although you will get blisters when you get there! But you were going there anyway.

Sometimes when I have used this parable, people try to reverse it and confuse it and complicate it. They say, "What if you come along and offer me a ride to PUC when I was going to Las Vegas?" Or, "What if you offer me a ride to Las Vegas when I was going to PUC?" Or, "What if I *think* I'm going to PUC but really I'm headed for Las Vegas?" Or, "What if you *think* you are going to take me to PUC but really you take me to Las Vegas?" And so on and on! But we know that God will never base His decision as to whether or not someone receives eternal salvation on what someone else does or doesn't do.

According to Scripture, God is a God of love, and, also according to Scripture, He is responsible for you being born into this world. It wasn't the devil, and it wasn't your parents. It was God. If those two ideas are true—that God is a God of love and He is responsible for our being born—then He would have to give every person an adequate chance for something better. And He does. Jesus is the Light that enlightens everyone who comes into the world (John 1:9).

Then the only thing that can determine whether you are going to PUC or Las Vegas is your own choice. No one else can decide that for you. And when it comes to your eternal salvation, you are guaranteed an adequate chance to accept eternal life. This doesn't mean that everyone has an equal chance. Those who have been raised in a Christian environment and know much of the things of God and heaven certainly have an advantage over those in the darkness of heathenism who never hear the name of Jesus. But everyone, at some time during his or her lifetime, will have an adequate opportunity to choose God.

In the judgment, no one will be able to legitimately point to another person and say, "He's the reason I'm not going to be saved." All will understand that they decided their destiny for themselves.

However, the fact that we don't hold the salvation of others in our hands doesn't mean that God can't use our hands to extend the offer of salvation to them. We can be channels of His working. We can be the means He uses to reach those who are willing to be reached. So we *can* have a part in the salvation of other people. We can hasten the process. We can help them get there sooner! We can save them many trials and heartaches and bruises along the way. We can bring them the peace of God years earlier than they would otherwise have received it.

Let's nail this down: our prayers can be a part of the process of hastening God's work in the lives of those around us.

"LEND ME THREE LOAVES"

One of the most beautiful passages of Scripture on the subject of intercessory prayer is found in Luke 11:5–8.

> He said unto them, Which of you shall have a friend, and shall go unto him at midnight, and say unto him, Friend, lend me three loaves; for a friend of mine in his journey is come to me, and I have nothing to set before him? And he from within shall answer and say, Trouble me not: the door is now shut, and my children are with me in bed; I cannot rise and give thee. I say unto you, Though he will not rise and give him, because he is his friend, yet because of his importunity he will rise and give him as many as he needeth.

Then follows Jesus' famous promise, "Ask, and it shall be given you; seek, and ye shall find," and so forth (verse 9). It was given in the context of this parable about praying for others.

Put yourself in the picture. You have a friend who has been traveling across the country. He comes to your house late at night, and he's hungry. But you have nothing to offer him. Your cupboard is bare. Your pantry is empty. Maybe you were planning to go grocery shopping tomorrow, but he's hungry *now*. It's midnight, and the 7-Eleven closed an hour ago. What are you going to do?

First, the question is *not* whether your friend will starve to death. The question is whether he will go to bed hungry. His *life* is not in your hands, but his *comfort* is.

So you hurry over to the pastor's house and knock on the door. The pastor and his family are asleep. The pastor is quite unhappy that you have awakened him in the middle of the night. Apparently, he doesn't even come to the front door. He just opens the bedroom window and calls out from upstairs, "Don't bother me. We're in bed asleep. The door is shut. Come back tomorrow."

But you stay right there. You say, "I have a friend who has come to me for help, and I have nothing to give him. You've *got* to help." And you persist in your appeal.

Do you think you could do that? Would you be intimidated by the fact that you were causing inconvenience to someone else? Or would you be so intent on getting something for your friend who is in need that you would persist in spite of the apparent dismissal?

Notice the three factors that enable you to continue pleading even in the face of obstacles. First, you have a friend who is in need. You're not asking this for yourself, but for someone else. That fact adds extra courage that would otherwise be missing.

Second, the one upon whose door you are knocking has what is needed. You know ahead of time that you will be able to get what you need for your friend from this source. The response is not, "I don't have any bread either. Go home and go to bed," but rather, "Don't bother me."

And finally, you and the pastor are friends! He may not seem very friendly right now, but sometimes the lack of politeness can be an indication of friendship, can't it? If you were some stranger, the pastor might be quicker to put his best foot forward—to play his official role. But since it's you, he trusts your friendship enough to say, "Don't bother me!" Have you ever had it happen that way?

So, you *are* friends, not only with the one *for* whom you seek the three loaves—but also with the one *from* whom you seek them. Notice how the midnight petitioner began his request: "*Friend,* lend me three loaves." There is an already established relationship here, which the one making the request is not afraid to depend upon.

Have you ever seen the little adage, "The test of friendship is not how you handle each other's words, but how you handle each other's silence"? Friends don't have to chatter constantly to know they are friends. They can be comfortable together even in silence. Is that true of your friendship with God? Are you comfortable with His silence?

Do you know Him well enough for that?

We are told that Jesus gave this parable by way of contrast, not comparison. There are times when God is silent for a time in order to test the genuineness of our desires and of our trust in Him, but He is willing to give, and He delights in responding to our requests. Andrew Murray quotes from this parable in his book on intercessory prayer and suggests that perhaps the reason Jesus used contrast to make His point was that He couldn't find anyone in real life whom He could use by way of comparison! Perhaps so. But because of the first three facts, the one seeking loaves at midnight comes to a definite conclusion. He says, "I have a friend in need; you have what this friend and I need; you and I are friends as well, and so I'm not leaving. I'm staying here until you produce the goods!"

Do you have a friend in need? Do you realize your own helplessness to meet his need? And do you know another Friend who has all power and all the resources of heaven and earth at His command? The assurance of Jesus' story is that you *can* go to your heavenly Friend and be assured of the help that the situation requires. The parable ends on a triumphant note: the one who sought for help at midnight was given as much help as he needed. "Never will one be told, I cannot help you. Those who beg at midnight for loaves to feed the hungry souls will be successful."[1]

Andrew Murray writes in his book *The Ministry of Intercession:* "If we will but believe in God and His faithfulness, intercession will become to us the very first thing we take refuge in when we seek blessing for others; and the very last thing for which we cannot find time."

This chapter is taken from Morris Venden's book, The Answer Is Prayer *(Nampa, Idaho: Pacific Press®, 1988). Used by permission.*

---

1. Ellen G. White, *Christ's Object Lessons*, 148.

Chapter 10

THE SONG OF MOSES AND THE LAMB

C. T. EVERSON, E. G. WHITE, AND C. F. ALEXANDER

Charles T. Everson preached a sermon titled "The Song of Moses and the Lamb" at a General Conference in the 1930s. With his widow's permission, I found his verbatim notes in his files. I've included with it excerpts from the chapter "The Death of Moses" in Patriarchs and Prophets, *and a poem on the death of Moses by Cecil Frances Alexander.*

Moses, who is in heaven now, may be watching as you read this sermon—what a wonderful thought! Moses is there because he chose to suffer affliction with the people of God rather than to enjoy the pleasures of Egypt—of sin—for a season. He could be a mummy today in a sarcophagus in Cairo, but he made the better choice. Moses' conversion inspires us anew with the desire to be born again.

And Moses went up from the plains of Moab unto the mountain of Nebo, to the top of Pisgah, that is over against Jericho. And the LORD shewed him all the land of Gilead, unto Dan, and all Naphtali, and the land of Ephraim, and Manasseh, and all the land of Judah, unto the utmost sea, and the south, and plain of the valley of Jericho, the city of palm trees, unto Zoar. And the LORD said unto him, This is the land which I sware unto Abraham, unto Isaac, and unto Jacob, saying, I will give it unto thy seed: I have caused thee to see it with thine eyes, but thou shalt not go over thither. So Moses the servant of the LORD died there in the land of Moab, according to the word of the LORD. And he buried him in a valley in the land of Moab, over against Bethpeor: but no man knoweth of his sepulchre unto this day (Deuteronomy 34:1–6).

The two great characters for the last days are Moses and Elijah. Moses, one of the leading prophets of all time, represents those who die and will be resurrected at Christ's second coming. Something about the song of Moses especially applies to God's people. The Bible says we will sing the song of Moses and the Lamb.

Moses, the man who talked to God face to face, would never have entered history except for his mother, Jochebed. "Pharaoh charged all his people, saying, Every son that is born ye shall cast into the river" (Exodus 1:22). When the decree was in full force, Moses was born. His mother kept him hid for three months at home and finally placed him in a basket floating on the bosom of the Nile. Pharaoh's daughter was the offspring of the child's greatest enemy, but God gave her a mother's love. It was love at first sight.

Moses' mother lived near the palace in a little house provided for her. She became a servant to her son, to win him for God. Near the Egyptian palace, with its black arts, witchcraft, spiritism of the deepest dye—without a preacher, without a Sabbath School, without a young people's society, without a church school—a lone woman, in the midnight darkness of Egypt, prayed and wept. Through her tears she taught him so well of the things of heaven that the dazzling splendor of Egypt could not attract him.

The throne, the greatest seat of authority and power in the world of his day, beckoned him. On the other hand, there stood a band of slaves that his mother had told him were his people. She took him out and showed him the Israelites, dressed only in their loincloths, with bandanna handkerchiefs around their heads, digging with their bare hands in the clay pits, their brown backs all cut up by the taskmaster's lash. A smell of garlic and onions lingered about them. Moses' mother told him, "These, my son, are your people."

"It can't be possible," he exclaimed. They were such a low stratum of humanity. But she had taught him so well that he chose that band of clay-digging slaves as his future companions for life. Rather than accepting the throne of Egypt with the greatest cultural minds of ancient times, he decided to suffer affliction with the people of God. He knew what the choice meant.

When your boy or girl comes to the great decision, and the world offers them position, pleasure, and honor, if only they will give up their faith, what weighs most with them? Do God's people look small, insignificant, and without a future? Remember that while we might not be a great people, Moses had but a downtrodden, clay-digging band of slaves to choose as his. And he joined them with all his heart. He loved them to the end and was never sorry that he made the decision.

NOT READY FOR THE TASK

A man with a high brow and intellectual face sits in the wilderness with a few paltry sheep around him. He looks strangely out of place, tending a few sheep that a lad could shepherd for pennies a day. Why was this great intellect holding a shepherd boy's job? Because he was not ready for his great task. He was a quick-tempered man who could whip out a dagger and stick it into a man's back and then bury his body in the sand. It took him forty years in the wilderness to learn his lesson—a long, desolate experience. Forty years, while the people of God cried for deliverance from the taskmaster's lash. But they must wait until Moses was ready. The sheep taught him, and when the forty years ended, God said of him, "He is the meekest man in all the earth."

Perhaps it seemed to you that your days were being irretrievably lost in your wilderness experience. But God has always been there, waiting in the burning bush to call you as soon as you have learned your lesson. And it did not take long, once Moses was ready, to deliver Israel.

After his great sacrifice, the people gave no response, no word of appreciation. People for whom he had forsaken everything responded with nothing but murmuring, backbiting, and faultfinding. He never could please them. They accused him of bringing them into the desert to let them die of thirst. When they became thirsty and their children cried for water, the great rabble arose like a storm cloud. Moses was alone. What could he do against ignorant, maddened slaves looking for stones to crush his skull? All he could do was flee to God for protection. No wonder Scripture says he talked to God as a man speaks to his friend. He would tell God that he must have water or they would soon hurl rocks at him. God said, "I will bring water out of the rock." And the people calmed down.

Then they milled around because they couldn't sow and reap in the sands of the desert. God rained down bread from heaven. But they complained about the manna that the angels eat and wished themselves back in Egypt with the garlic and onions. Their highest ideal seemed to be garlic and onions and Baal and licentiousness. Moses heard nothing from the people he had rescued from the hardest bondage but complaints, murmurings, and threats to kill him. "Not a thank you," says Moses, "have I heard from their lips." He came in among the congregation and thought to find a company of angels ready for translation.

We have expected great appreciation for the sacrifice we made to take up the faith and were heartbroken when we found ourselves criticized, backbitten, with no end of faultfinding, and apparent lack of sympathy. Disappointed, perhaps we exclaimed, "Is it possible that this is really God's people? Why, the world appreciates me more than they do!" Don't forget the song of Moses and the Lamb.

Not only was Moses unappreciated and criticized, but his life was in peril again and again. When tempted to leave the people of God, I wish you would keep something in mind. The people of Israel finally sank so low and became so rebellious and licentious and faultfinding that apparently God became discouraged with them, and said, "I will end this travesty on religion. I will sweep these ungrateful wretches off the earth. I will destroy all, including Aaron." The Lord said to Moses, "Let me alone . . . that I may consume them: and I will make of thee a great nation." Moses might have thought, *You're right. You can't make anything of these lowbrows, this garlic-loving, uncultured mob. With me as the beginning of a new people, You are going to get somewhere. I have culture, education, and everything You need to found a real nation upon.*

Some people leave the faith because they lose a job in the church. Suppose God gave the leaders of this kind of people such an offer. Wouldn't they jump at it? But they will never sing the song of Moses and the Lamb. Moses wasn't thinking of himself, his fame, or his honor. He had given up everything for God years before. Long before, he had united his heart and soul to his people, had learned to love them because they were God's people. Now he would not give them up. His love for them was like God's love for unworthy human beings.

Immediately, Moses began to intercede for them, reminding God of His love for them and how he could not bear to be separated from them. Over and over, he repeated it, but his case was desperate. God's decision to destroy the Hebrews seemed apparently irrevocable. But Moses held on, pleading. He placed before God every reason he could find for urging Him to save them. Yet they were a people who again and again were ready to take up rocks at a moment's notice and stone him, leaving his body rotting in the wilderness for the vultures to devour.

Are you prepared to sing the song of Moses and the Lamb? Moses loved a people a hundred times more unlovable than those we see today. He would not give them up for all the world. Do you admire Moses' love for God's people? Or do you allow some small insult to drive you away from loving His people today? Remember the song of Moses.

PLEADING WITH GOD

Finally, he saw that his pleading apparently could not change God's decision. He did not question God's stand. Their sin was great. Moses knew that. They had attributed to the golden calf their deliverance from Egypt. They were saying that the god of their enemies was the great power that rescued them from Egyptian slavery.

Moses had one thing left, and he didn't hesitate to use it. He had his name in the book of life. As a last resort, he threw his own eternal life in the balances to save the people. God could not prevent him from doing it. Everyone has the right to choose life or death. The Lord cannot take that away from anyone. You will notice a dash in the middle of Exodus 32:32. It stands for a pause. Moses is sobbing out his heart; he knows how impossible it has been. God may accept his challenge and wipe him out. But he says, "God, please forgive, forgive I pray Thee—or blot me out with the people." Rather than lose Moses, God forgave the people's sin and saved them.

Because of his love for his people, Moses was willing to go down to destruction. It was an echo of Calvary—one man willing to give up his eternal life for others who were apparently his enemies. Some have been willing to give up *this* life for others, but Moses was willing to forfeit perpetual life. No wonder Scripture links his name with Christ's forever. "And they sing the song of Moses . . . and . . . the Lamb."

Are you offended at the slightest affront, ready to shake the dust off your feet and leave God's people today? Does criticism of God's people by enemies and offshoots turn you against the church? Or, like Moses of old, can you say, "They are God's people, and I will stay by them until the heavenly Canaan appears"?

However, a great disappointment did come to Moses. When the people crowded around him, threatening to stone him, he lost himself for a minute and smote the rock. "Ye rebels; must we fetch you water out of this rock?" He took the glory to himself. Immediately after he had uttered the words, he realized his great mistake. God said, "You have failed to sanctify Me in the people's presence. You shall not go into the Promised Land."

Our Lord holds leaders responsible for much more than He does the people. If you are anxious to be a leader, remember that God places greater accountability on you than on others. But Moses had his heart set on going into the Promised Land. It was the one thought that had cheered him when Israel railed against him. Wait until they see that marvelous country flowing with milk and honey. Will it not be glorious at last to hear them shout for joy?

But the consolation was denied him. It was more than he could bear. All looked forlorn and dark. But he still had hope. He decided to talk it over with God. Moses knew what prayer could do.

So he began to plead with God: "God, let me go over and see the goodly land. Let me go over, God. O Father, let me go over. You know how hard pressed I have been with these people all these years, and especially on that fatal day. O Father, let me go over and see the goodly land!"

Moses had such a hold on God's heart and he tugged so hard at His heartstrings that the Lord could not let him go on praying or He might have given in. So He had to tell Moses to stop asking. When Moses learned that, he sobbed out, "But must I die in this land?" That same day the command came to Moses, "Get thee up . . . unto mount Nebo, . . . and behold the land of Canaan, which I give unto the children of Israel for a possession: and die in the mount whither thou goest up, and be gathered unto thy people" (Deuteronomy 32:49, 50).

"Moses had often left the camp, in obedience to the divine summons, to commune with God; but he was now to depart on a new and mysterious errand. He must go forth to resign his life into the hands of his Creator. Moses knew that he was to die alone; no earthly friend would be permitted to minister to him in his last hours. There was a mystery and awfulness about the scene before him, from which his heart shrank. The severest trial was his separation from the people of his care and love—the people with whom his interest and his life had so long been united. But he had learned to trust in God, and with unquestioning faith he committed himself and his people to His love and mercy.

"For the last time Moses stood in the assembly of his people. Again the Spirit of God rested upon him, and in the most sublime and touching language he pronounced a blessing upon each of the tribes, closing with a benediction upon them all."

"As the people gazed upon the aged man, so soon to be taken from them, they recalled, with a new and deeper appreciation, his parental tenderness, his wise counsels, and his untiring labors. How often, when their sins had invited the just judgments of God, the prayers of Moses had prevailed with Him to spare them! Their grief was heightened by remorse. They bitterly remembered that their own perversity had provoked Moses to the sin for which he must die."

UP THE MOUNTAIN ALONE

"Moses turned from the congregation, and in silence and alone made his way up the mountainside. He went to 'the mountain of Nebo, to the top of Pisgah.' Upon that lonely height he stood, and gazed with undimmed eye upon the scene spread out before him. Far away to the west lay the blue waters of the Great Sea; in the north, Mount Hermon stood out against the sky; to the east was the table-land of Moab, . . . and away to the south stretched the desert of their long wanderings. . . .

". . . Notwithstanding all that God had wrought for [Israel], notwithstanding [Moses'] own prayers and labors, only two of all the adults in the vast army that left Egypt had been found so faithful that they could enter the Promised Land. As Moses reviewed the result of his labors, his life of trial and sacrifice seemed to have been almost in vain.

"Yet he did not regret the burdens he had borne. He knew that his mission and work were of God's own appointing. . . . He felt that he had made a wise decision in choosing to suffer affliction with the people of God, rather than to enjoy the pleasures of sin for a season.

"As he looked back upon his experience as a leader of God's people, one wrong act marred the record. If that transgression could be blotted out, he felt that he would not shrink from death. He was assured that repentance, and faith in the promised Sacrifice, were all that God required, and again Moses confessed his sin and implored pardon in the name of Jesus.

"And now a panoramic view of the Land of Promise was presented to him. Every part of the country was spread out before him, not faint and uncertain in the dim distance, but standing out clear, distinct, and beautiful to his delighted vision. In this scene it was presented, not as it then appeared, but as it would become, with God's blessing upon it, in the possession of Israel. He seemed to be looking upon a second Eden. There were mountains clothed with cedars of Lebanon, hills gray with olives and fragrant with the odor of the vine, wide green plains bright with flowers and rich in fruitfulness, here the palm trees of the tropics, there waving fields of wheat and barley, sunny valleys musical with the ripple of brooks and the song of birds, goodly cities and fair gardens, lakes rich in 'the abundance of the seas,' grazing flocks upon the hillsides, and even amid the rocks the wild bee's hoarded treasures. . . .

"Moses saw the chosen people established in Canaan. . . . He had a view of their history after the settlement of the Promised Land; the long, sad story of their apostasy. . . . He saw them, because of their sins, dispersed among the heathen, . . . captives in strange lands. He saw them restored to the land of their fathers, and at last brought under the dominion of Rome.

"He was permitted to look down the stream of time and behold the first advent of our Saviour. He saw Jesus as a babe in Bethlehem. He heard the voices of the angelic host break forth in the glad song of praise to God and peace on earth. He beheld in the heavens the star guiding the Wise Men of the East to Jesus. . . . He beheld Christ's humble life in Nazareth, His ministry of love and sympathy and healing, His rejection by a proud, unbelieving nation. . . . He saw Jesus upon Olivet as with weeping He bade farewell to the city of His love. As Moses beheld the final rejection of that people . . . his heart was wrung with anguish, and bitter tears fell from his eyes, in sympathy with the sorrow of the Son of God.

"He followed the Saviour to Gethsemane, and beheld the agony in the garden, the betrayal, the mockery and scourging—the crucifixion. . . . Grief, indignation, and horror filled the heart of Moses as he viewed the hypocrisy and satanic hatred manifested by the Jewish nation against their Redeemer. . . . He heard Christ's agonizing cry, 'My God, My God, why hast thou forsaken Me?' Mark 15:34. He saw Him lying in Joseph's new tomb. The darkness of hopeless despair seemed to enshroud the world. But he looked again, and beheld Him coming forth a conqueror, and ascending to heaven escorted by adoring angels and leading a multitude of captives. He saw the shining gates open to receive Him, and the host of heaven with songs of triumph welcoming their Commander. And it was there revealed to him that he himself would be one who should attend the Saviour, and open to Him the everlasting gates. As he looked upon the scene, his countenance shone with a holy radiance. How small appeared the trials and sacrifices of his life when compared with those of the Son of God! . . . He rejoiced that he had been permitted, even in a small measure, to be partaker in the sufferings of Christ. . . .

"[Then Moses witnessed the early Christian church, the Dark Ages, and the day to which you and I have come.] . . . He saw the second coming of Christ in glory, the righteous dead raised to immortal life, and the living saints translated without seeing death, and together ascending with songs of gladness to the City of God.

"Still another scene opens to his view—the earth freed from the curse, lovelier than the fair Land of Promise so lately spread out before him. There is no sin, and death cannot enter. There the nations of the saved find their eternal home. With joy unutterable Moses looks upon the scene—the fulfillment of a more glorious deliverance than his brightest hopes have ever pictured. Their earthly wanderings forever past, the Israel of God have at last entered the goodly land.

"Again the vision faded, and his eyes rested upon the land of Canaan as it spread out in the distance. Then, like a tired warrior, he lay down to rest. 'So Moses the servant of the Lord died there in the land of Moab, according to the word of the Lord. And He buried him in a valley in the land of Moab, over against Beth-peor: but no man knoweth of his sepulcher' " (Deuteronomy 34:5, 6).

By Nebo's lonely mountain, on this side Jordan's wave
In a vale in the land of Moab there lies a lonely grave;
And no man knows that sepulcher, and no man saw it e'er;
For the angels of God upturn'd the sod and laid the dead man
   there.

That was the grandest funeral that ever pass'd on earth;
But no man heard the trampling, or saw the train go forth:
Noiselessly as the daylight comes when the night is down,
And the crimson streak on ocean's cheek grows into the great
   sun.

Noiselessly as the springtime, her crown of verdure weaves,
And all the trees on all the hills open their thousand leaves;
So without sound of music, or voice of them that wept,
Silently down from the mountain's crown the great procession
   swept.
Perchance the bald old eagle, on gray Beth-peor's height,
Out from his lonely eyrie look'd on the wondrous sight.
Perchance the lion stalking, still shuns that hallowed spot;
For beast and bird have seen and heard that which man
   knoweth not.

But, when the warrior dieth, his comrades in the war,
With arms reversed and muffled drums, follow his funeral car;
They show the banners taken, they tell his battles won,
And after him lead his masterless steed, while peals the
   minute-gun.

Amid the noblest of the land we lay the sage to rest,
And give the bard an honor'd place, with costly marble drest,
In great minster transept where lights like glories fall,
And the sweet choir sings, and the organ rings along the
   emblazoned wall.

This was the truest warrior that ever buckled sword;
This the most gifted poet that ever breathed a word;
And never earth's philosopher traced, with his golden pen,
On the deathless page, truths half so sage, as he wrote down
    for men.

And had he not high honor? The hillside for a pall!
To lie in state, while angels wait, with stars for tapers tall,
And the dark rock-pines like tossing plumes over his bier to
    wave,
And God's own hand, in that lonely land, to lay him in the
    grave!—

In that strange grave without a name, whence his uncoffin'd
    clay
Shall break again, O wondrous thought!—*before* the judgment
    day,
And stand, with glory wrapped around, on the hills he never
    trod.
And speak of the strife that won our life with the incarnate
    Son of God.

Moses died of a broken heart. His strength was still unimpaired,
his sight perfect. But God, too, was brokenhearted when Moses died.
He sent Jesus to bring Moses to heaven, loving him so dearly He
could not wait, but said, "Jesus, raise him up and bring him to Me
that I may clasp him in My arms."

Later, when circumstances looked discouraging to Christ, God
sent Moses to speak words of comfort to His soul. The Exodus leader
had been alone also in life. On the mountaintop he sat beside Jesus
and repeated the story of his great disappointment and how his sacrifice for the people brought nothing but heartbreak, with little appreciation. Christ took courage and went forward to save you and me. I
love Moses for the great comfort he gave to my Jesus when He needed

the help of a heart that understood. No wonder those two hearts that were broken will beat together in that blessed country. And we shall sing the song of Moses and the Lamb.

Will you be there to sing that song? All heaven will stop to listen as we unite our voices in the song that makes angels stand spellbound. What a thrill that will be when Christ raises His hand and the great chorus begins to sing in the land where song was born. On the sea of glass mingled with fire, as the glory of God shines into the calm crystal sea, will you join in that great chorus at last? Now is the time to learn that wonderful song of experience. Are you ready to sing the song of Moses and the Lamb? Are you ready to love the unlovable, love the ungrateful, love the unappreciative, even those who seek to stone you? Through the great lanes of eternity, the smallest planets on the outer limits of the universe will stop and listen and wonder at a people who could love and forgive unto the end. That is singing the song of Moses and the Lamb.

O lonely grave in Moab's land! O dark Beth-peor's hill!
Speak to these curious hearts of ours, and teach them to be still.
God hath His mysteries of grace, ways that we cannot tell,
He hides them deep, like the hidden sleep of him He loved so well.

This chapter is taken from Morris Venden's book From Exodus to Advent *(Nashville: Southern Publishing Association, 1980). Under public domain. The chapter is based on notes for a sermon preached by Charles T. Everson; substantial quotations from Ellen G. White's* Patriarchs and Prophets *(Mountain View, Calif.: Pacific Press®, 1958), 470–477; and the poem "The Burial of Moses" by Cecil Frances Alexander.*

Appendix A

PARABLES ON CONVERSION

VARIOUS AUTHORS

CADAVER AND FRIENDS
by Morris Venden

> *You . . . who were dead in trespasses and sins.*
> —Ephesians 2:1

Two students go off to school to study medicine. One of the first things they are introduced to is the anatomy lab. In this lab, there is a heavy silence. It's kind of cold, and things are really dead there!

But these medical students are anxious to make a good showing, so they analyze the situation. They notice that there is a good deal of unity in the lab. No fights seem to be going on among the "patients"; no one is vying for the highest place. They're all in the same position.

As the medical students consider the situation, they become convinced that what these individuals need is to grow. After futile attempts to get them to grow and after trying to get them to exercise, they decide that there is an even deeper problem.

One day they wonder if the problem of these people in the lab is that they don't have any fellowship. But that turns out to be a dead-end street, for the "patients" there refuse to be sociable. The students even try to develop a statement of mission for Cadaver and his friends, but it is ignored.

In the end, the medical students discover, to their dismay, that all the people in the lab have a common problem: they're not breathing. And another problem, that came even earlier, is that they're not eating, either. And the reason they're not eating or breathing is that they are not even alive!

THE DEATH OF BEN TRYING
by Bill Gravestock

Not by works of righteousness which we have done, but according to his mercy he saved us, by the washing of regeneration, and renewing of the Holy Ghost; which he shed on us abundantly through Jesus Christ our Saviour; that being justified by his grace, we should be made heirs according to the hope of eternal life.

—Titus 3:5–7

This story begins and ends in Mercy Hospital—in the intensive care ward. The patient's name is Ben Trying. He'd *been* trying to be a Christian. He'd *been* trying to be good. He'd *been* trying to believe, to have faith, to break through. But it seemed useless, hopeless. Now he lay flat on his back with but a few brief hours to live. To him, every moment was very precious. He knew that he was breathing on borrowed time. He had no one to help him prepare for eternity except his three religious sisters. All were professed Christians. Each had come to comfort and console their dear brother in this tragic moment of crisis and grief. Maybe they could help him break through and believe before it was too late. Even now, they waited in the lobby of the intensive care ward to see their dying brother.

The nurse whispered to one of the sisters, Miss Nebulous N. Tangible. She quietly followed the nurse into the room of her dear, despairing brother, where she was told that she had three minutes. As she sat by her brother's bedside and looked into his eyes, she knew that he was without God and without hope. He clutched her hand and moaned, "Please, Sis, help me to break through. . . . I don't . . . have much time. . . . Help me to believe. . . . Please help me!"

How could he be helped? What could she say? She took a deep breath and began to speak. "Ben! Ben, listen to me. You must give your heart to Jesus quickly."

Ben stared at her in disbelief. He moved his hand over his heart and looked puzzled.

"You must reach out your hand and take His and then invite Him into your heart. You must behold the Lamb and surrender your will."

Ben's expression conveyed confusion, so she continued. "You must fall on the Rock. You must repent of your sins and then accept freely His robe of righteousness. This is your covering—your wedding garment. It is yours, Ben, when you repent and believe."

Beads of sweat rolled off Ben's tired, worn face. His head lay back on the pillow as he stared hopelessly at the ceiling. A mournful sigh escaped his lips as he trembled in despair. The nurse came in and whispered, "Miss Nebulous, your time is up."

The second sister, Miss Solid Ann Concrete, made her way into her brother's room and sat at his bedside. Before she could say anything, Ben looked frantically at her and with great effort forced out these words: "Oh, Sis, please help me. . . . Help me to believe. . . . I'm trying . . . to break through, . . . but I can't. . . . I can't."

She leaned over and looked into his face. It portrayed the anxiousness of his heart. She then took his trembling hand and said, "Ben, I can only tell you what the Bible says about the kind of people who will go to heaven. Their behavior will be in distinct contrast to that of the world. If you want to be there, . . . well, it's up to you. But in order for you to have hope and in order for you to be a Christian, you must first renounce your old life of sin—your life of wickedness and selfishness. Your social habits—your behavior and conversation—must be drastically changed. Everything you do has got to go. It's evil. It's no good.

"I have to tell you the truth. You must give up your gambling. Stop smoking. Stop drinking. Quit going to those terrible bars and nightclubs. Change your habit patterns. Don't associate with your old friends; make new ones. Lose all that weight. Quit being a glutton. Make your body a fit place for the Lord to dwell. Allow only good and uplifting and ennobling thoughts to enter your mind. Stop reading those vile magazines and stories. Instead, read the Bible. Fill your mind with things that are pure and lovely. Dwell on things in heaven. Love the Lord and hate evil with perfect hatred and . . . and . . . Ben! Ben! . . . Are you listening? . . . Ben? . . . Are you all right? Nurse! Nurse!"

Ben gasped for breath. He choked and gagged. The nurse quickly took his pulse. "He's almost gone. Could you wait outside please?"

Moments later, the nurse beckoned to the last sister. "Are you Ben's other sister?" she asked.

"Yes, I am."

"You don't have much time," the nurse said, "and neither does he."

"I understand, nurse. Thank you so very much."

Sitting beside her precious brother, Miss Faith N. Christ took his hand and prayed silently that her words would be a savor of life unto life to poor Ben, her wandering, lost baby brother. She looked into his eyes with hope and courage and said, "Ben, are you ready to die?"

"No, . . . I'm not ready, . . . Sis, . . . but I'm trying to be ready. . . . I'm . . . trying to break through. . . . I'm trying to believe, . . . Sis." He wrung his hands and wept as he sighed and shook his head. "It's no use. . . . I just can't believe. . . . I just can't break through. I've tried as hard as I can, but it's no use, . . . no use."

Faith leaned toward his ear as he lay there motionless. "My dear brother Ben, I understand your predicament. Would you just be still for a few minutes? Just be very quiet and listen. That's all I ask for you to do—just listen."

As soon as Ben was calm, Faith began to speak. She didn't urge him to try harder to believe. Instead, she gave him the assurance that God the Father had loved him in Jesus Christ. She began to tell him the good news—the glad tidings. "Ben," she said, "while you were His enemy, the Father loved you and chose you to be with Him where He is. He spared not His only Son for you. All of heaven was emptied and went bankrupt for you. He has given all of the accumulated and hoarded love and wealth of eternity in the gift of Jesus, His Son. You have been redeemed, forgiven, and accepted in Jesus.

"Two thousand years ago, when the fullness of the time had come, God the Son, your Savior, Jesus, left heaven because, despite all of its stupendous glory, He didn't want to stay there while you were lost. He whom angels loved and worshiped stepped down from His exalted throne to come to this dark planet Earth. At heaven's appointed hour, He was born in a lowly stable for you, Ben. When He grew up, He suffered shame and humiliation as the rejected One in order that you might be the accepted one. For your sake He became poor that through His poverty you might be rich. He was treated the way you deserve that you might be treated the way He deserves. He wore the crown of thorns that you might wear the crown of life. He died for you, and now He offers to take your sins and give you His righteousness.

"If you give yourself to Him and accept Him as your Savior, then, sinful as your life may have been, for His sake, you are accounted righteous. Christ's character stands in place of your character, and you are accepted before God as if you had not sinned. More than that, Christ changes the heart. He abides in your heart by faith."

Ben heard the everlasting gospel. Faith was kindled in his heart. He saw, through the illumination of the Holy Spirit, that he was accepted because Jesus was acceptable. He saw that he was pleasing in God's sight because Jesus was altogether pleasing—"This is my beloved Son, in whom I am well pleased" (Matthew 3:17). He grasped the simple truth that Jesus was his personal Representative and his Righteousness at the Father's right hand. He realized now that the question was not "Will God accept me?" In the light of the gospel, the question was *"Will I accept the fact that I've been accepted?"* He comprehended the amazing discovery that the very fact he was a sinner entitled him to come to Jesus.

Then he had no more questions, no more doubts. The Holy Spirit illuminated his mind, and little by little, the chain of evidence was joined together. In Jesus—bruised, mocked, and hanging upon the cross—he saw the Lamb of God who takes away the sin of the world. Hope flooded his soul. Gratitude swelled in his heart for Jesus. Tears rolled down his cheeks. Joy filled his soul. He was melted and subdued, and a smile broke upon his face as he said, "I see it. . . . I see that it . . . was . . . for me. I accept it. I believe."

That was Ben's last message of mercy. But it was enough. Faith in Christ through the everlasting gospel was his peace and hope.

LEONARD, THE UPTIGHT WOLF
by Ken McFarland

If any man be in Christ, he is a new creature: old things are passed away; behold, all things are become new.
—2 Corinthians 5:17

Leonard the wolf was starting to get uncomfortably uptight. His folks, who of course were also wolves, kept hanging around this flock of sheep that lived not too far away. Now, wolves are expected to hang around sheep—but only for dietary reasons. What really worried Leonard was his folks' weird notion about trying to imitate sheep, about wanting everyone to think they were sheep too. They even wore sheepskins!

To make matters worse, every weekend Leonard's folks made him get all dressed up in his own sheepskin. Then they snarled him off to the sheepfold, where one of the assistant shepherds droned on and on about how to be a better sheep.

Now, some real sheep happened to be members of the flock. They seemed to actually get something out of the assistant shepherd's talk. But there were also plenty of wolves there, dressed up in their own sheepskins, also pretending to be sheep and hoping to fool the sheep—

and even the other wolves. Not Leonard! He could spot them as soon as the meeting let out. It was easy. Most of them went home, took off their sheepskins, and lived like wolves the rest of the week.

Strangely enough, Leonard's own folks wore their sheepskins all the time—at least, Leonard never saw them without their sheepskins. Maybe they thought if they wore them long enough, they might someday turn into sheep.

Leonard's mom and dad seemed desperately eager to make sure he acted just like a sheep, even though he rather enjoyed being a wolf and detested having to be a sheep. His folks sent him off to sheep school, even though they could have saved piles of money by sending him to the cheaper wolf schools all around.

Sheep school was a full-on bummer. Leonard had to take sheep lessons there. Ugh! And they had about thirty zillion "Do" and "Don't" sheep rules. He had to read the Shepherd's Manual and talk to the Shepherd, even though Leonard had never even seen the Shepherd and sometimes wondered if He really existed. He had to go out among the wolves to distribute little sheep pamphlets to convince other wolves to become sheep. He had to go to all the sheep meetings and study the Big Weekend Sheep Course each week. And worst of all, the things he was *not* supposed to do were all the things that wolves love to do—things like running around at night with other young wolves of the neighborhood, drinking wolfshine, going out with cute little foxes, watching tele-wolf, smoking wolfawanna, and listening to their favorite rock-n-howl group. Sheep school was unreal.

At sheep school, just as at the big, weekend sheepfold meetings, some of the students—maybe just a few—were real sheep. They were always talking about the Chief Shepherd, reading His Manual, eating grass, and smiling. They really seemed to groove on it. They made Leonard nervous.

Most of Leonard's close friends were like him—wolves who just wore their sheepskins because they had to. When they were together by themselves, they would drop the skins and rap about being forced to live like dumb sheep. As far as they could tell, the whole idea of being a sheep was, "If it feels good, don't do it. If it tastes good, spit it out. If it's fun, stop it!" And they were supposed to love the Chief Shepherd when in fact they almost hated Him—this killjoy in the sky; this celestial wet blanket whose Manual was hard to read and who was dead set against fun. "I'd like to just bag the whole thing," Leonard said one day, "and get out of this prison and have some real fun—you know, just let it all fang out, like the wolves over at the wolf school."

One day one of the sheep in Leonard's class overheard Leonard and his friends talking this way. After the others had gone, she walked over to Leonard and sat down beside him. "Want to talk about it?" she asked.

Well, why not? Leonard thought—even though he knew that since she was a real sheep, she couldn't possibly understand how he felt. But the sheep, Wendy, listened carefully as he poured out his frustrations.

"Leonard," she said when he had completely unburdened himself, "I know exactly how you feel. You see, until a couple of years ago, I was a wolf too."

Leonard's ears pointed sharply.

"I grew up like you," Wendy continued, "being forced to live like a sheep and hating every minute. My folks were like yours—wolves who just wore sheepskins, even though they probably were really trying to be sheep.

"Finally, I couldn't take it any longer. I felt I just had to get away, find myself, and get my head together. So I left everything. I left the sheep school, the sheepfold, my own pen at home—everything. I ran off and joined a huge pack of wolves a long way away. I had a great time for a while, doing just whatever I wanted to do.

"But pretty soon I found out that doing my own thing wasn't really as much fun as I had always figured it would be. Not that some of the things I was into weren't fun—they were. But the fun was only a half inch deep and lasted only about two minutes before it fizzled out. And I'd still be empty inside.

"And some of the things I'd been told were supposed to be a real blast ended up with a pretty big price tag on them. Someone told me that if I shot spider venom directly into my veins, I'd feel like the greatest wolf who ever lived. That turned out to be a real wipeout.

"Finally, when my money ran out, my friends did too. I had tried everything. My health was almost gone. There were no new thrills left, and the fun was over. There was this hollow place somewhere inside that I couldn't seem to fill—this itch I couldn't scratch.

"One night I decided to go out and run in front of a car and end it all. But somehow, before I did, I just happened to start flipping through the Chief Shepherd's Manual. No one made me do it this time. It was just something I felt I wanted to do.

"And was I ever amazed! I expected to find big lists of all those rules they had laid on us at sheep school inside. Instead, I found the most beautiful story I'd ever heard. It told about a time long ago when there were no wolves at all except for one great wolf who hated the Chief Shepherd. This great wolf attacked the Shepherd's flock of sheep and turned them all into wolves. From that time on, all of us have been separated from the Chief Shepherd. So it's no wonder we find ourselves enjoying the things wolves enjoy.

"But the Chief Shepherd still loved us, and He became a Lamb and came down and died for us so that any wolf who wants to can become a lamb too and have a chance to live forever in a place filled with green pastures and still waters.

"Well, Leonard, I read and read until I couldn't stay awake anymore. But by the time I fell asleep that night, I had found what I had been looking for all along. I had found the best Friend in all the world. I found Someone who loved me instead of condemning me—Someone who wanted to make me happier than I had ever dared to dream. And to think that all that time in sheep school I had been running away from Him!

"After that night, I spent all the time I could trying to learn more about the Chief Shepherd. And the more I talked to Him and read about Him, the more I noticed something very strange happening.

"Somehow, I noticed that I no longer enjoyed doing the things that wolves are supposed to enjoy. And I was getting really excited about the things that used to be such a drag—the things sheep do. And then one day I found out why. I discovered, Leonard, that I had become a sheep! Not just a wolf wearing a sheepskin—a real sheep. And, Leonard, you just can't believe how happy I am."

Leonard listened to Wendy for several hours and knew that she had discovered something he desperately wanted. That evening he went home and found a quiet place where he could be alone and pour out his heart to the Chief Shepherd. And before he dozed off to sleep that night, he threw away his sheepskin.

He wouldn't be needing it anymore.

The parables on conversion in this appendix are taken from the book by Morris Venden Modern Parables: Stories That Make Spiritual Truths Come Alive *(Nampa, Idaho: Pacific Press®, 1994). Used by permission.*

PONDER THIS . . .

ELLEN G. WHITE

"Many are inquiring, '*How* am I to make the surrender of myself to God?' You desire to give yourself to Him, but you are weak in moral power, in slavery to doubt, and controlled by the habits of your life of sin. Your promises and resolutions are like ropes of sand. You cannot control your thoughts, your impulses, your affections. The knowledge of your broken promises and forfeited pledges weakens your confidence in your own sincerity, and causes you to feel that God cannot accept you; but you need not despair. What you need to understand is the true force of the will. *This is the governing power in the nature of man, the power of decision, or of choice.* Everything depends on the right action of the *will [power of choice].* The *power of choice* God has given to men; it is theirs to exercise. You cannot change your heart, you cannot of yourself give to God its affections; but you can choose to *serve Him.* You can give Him your *will [power of choice];* He will then work in you to *will [choose]* and to do according to His good pleasure. Thus your whole nature will be brought under the control of the Spirit of Christ; your affections will be centered upon Him, your thoughts will be in harmony with Him. . . .

". . . Many will be lost while hoping and desiring to be Christians. They do not come to the point of yielding the *will [power of choice]* to God. They do not now choose to be Christians.

"Through the right exercise of the *will [power of choice]*, an entire change may be made in your life. By yielding up your *will [power of choice]* to Christ, you ally yourself with the power that is above all principalities and powers. You will have strength from above to hold you steadfast, and thus through constant surrender to God you will be enabled to live the new life, even the life of faith."—Ellen G. White, *Steps to Christ*, 47, 48; emphasis supplied.

"All true obedience comes from the heart. It was heart work with Christ. And if we consent, He will so identify Himself with our thoughts and aims, so blend our hearts and minds into conformity to His will, that when obeying Him we shall be but carrying out our own impulses. The will, refined and sanctified, will find its highest delight in doing His service. When we know God as it is our privilege to know Him, our life will be a life of continual obedience. Through an appreciation of the character of Christ, through communion with God, sin will become hateful to us."—Ellen G. White, *The Desire of Ages* (Mountain View, Calif.: Pacific Press®, 1940), 668.

Appendix C

VICTORY IN CHRIST

W. W. PRESCOTT

For a long time, I tried to gain the victory over sin, but I failed. I have since learned the reason. Instead of doing the part which God expects me to do and which I can do, I was trying to do God's part, which He does not expect me to do, and which I cannot do. Primarily, my part is not to win the victory, but to receive the victory which has already been won for me by Jesus Christ.

"But," you will ask, "does not the Bible speak about soldiers, and a warfare, and a fight?" Yes, it certainly does. "Are we not told that we must strive to enter in?" We surely are. "Well, what then?" Only this: that we should be sure for what we are fighting, and for what we are to strive.

Christ as a man fought the battle of life, and conquered. As my personal Representative, He won this victory for me, and so His word to me is, "Be of good cheer; I have overcome the world." I can therefore say with deep gratitude, "Thanks be to God, which giveth us the victory through our Lord Jesus Christ." My difficulty was due to this: that I did not give heed to the fact that victory is a gift already won and ready to be bestowed upon all who are willing to receive it. I assumed the responsibility of trying to win what He had already won for me. This led me into failure.

This victory is inseparable from Christ Himself, and when I learned how to receive Christ as my victory through union with

Him, I entered upon a new experience. I do not mean to say that I have not had any conflicts and that I have not made any mistakes. Far from it. But my conflicts have been when influences were brought to bear upon me to induce me to lose my confidence in Christ as my personal Savior and to separate from Him. My mistakes have been made when I have allowed something to come in between me and Him, to prevent me from looking into His blessed face with the look of faith. When I fix my eyes upon the enemy, or upon the difficulties, or upon myself and my past failures, I lose heart and fail to receive the victory. Therefore, "Looking Unto Jesus" is my motto.

The fight which I am to fight is "the good fight of faith," but the weapons of this warfare are not of the flesh. I do not believe in myself, and therefore, I have no confidence in my own power to overcome evil. I hear Him saying to me, "My power is made perfect in weakness," and so I surrender my whole being to be under His control, allowing Him to work in me "both to will and to work," and when I act upon the faith that He will do this in the way of victory, He does not disappoint me.

"Victory in Christ" is taken from W. W. Prescott's booklet by the same name (Hagerstown, Md.: Review and Herald®, 1987). Used with permission.

Appendix D

CONVERSION QUESTIONNAIRE

I created the following questionnaire and used it in several of the churches I pastored as an aid to my study on the subject of conversion. I have included it in this book for the benefit of those who may wish to use it in studies of their own.

1. Have you ever been converted? If so, continue through question 25. If not, skip to question 26.
2. At what age were you converted?
3. Are you still a born-again Christian?
4. Have you been baptized? At what age?
5. In what circumstances were you converted?
   - ❏ at a public meeting
   - ❏ responding to an altar call
   - ❏ with a small group or another person
   - ❏ alone
6. Did you come from Christian roots?
7. Did you have a Christian education?
8. Which best describes you before your conversion?
   - ❏ a moral person
   - ❏ a rebel
   - ❏ an open sinner

9. What best describes your conversion?
   - ❑ a sudden experience
   - ❑ a gradual process
10. Was a crisis involved?
11. Did you have a great sense of need? If so, on what level?
    - ❑ sinful condition
    - ❑ sinful behavior
    - ❑ problems of life
    - ❑ search for truth
    - ❑ contrast between yourself and Jesus
12. Was there some point of truth that led to your conversion when you understood it for the first time?
13. What best describes your conversion?
    - ❑ more emotional
    - ❑ more intellectual
14. Had you prayed to be converted?
15. Was someone else praying for your conversion?
16. Did you have a devotional life before conversion?
17. Did you have a devotional life after conversion?
18. Before your conversion, did you know that you were unconverted?
19. Did your moral behavior change at conversion?
20. Are you a strong-willed person?
21. Before your conversion, were you ever brought to the point of conversion only to turn away from it?
22. Before your conversion, were you aware of any particular sin that you were unwilling to give up?
23. Have you ever been converted and lost the experience? Did you understand why?
24. Have you ever had a part in someone else's conversion?
25. Do you often think and talk of Jesus?
26. Do you understand what conversion is?
27. Do you consider conversion important?
28. Have you ever been disgusted by public appeals or altar calls?

29. What do you think is the essence of Christianity?
   - ❑ correct behavior
   - ❑ correct doctrinal beliefs
   - ❑ a relationship with Christ
30. Do you come from Christian roots?
31. Do you believe in the reality of God?
32. Do you accept the unique Christian concept that everyone needs a Savior?
33. What do you consider yourself to be?
   - ❑ a good, moral person
   - ❑ a rebel
   - ❑ an open sinner
34. Do you have a desire for something spiritually better in your life?
35. Do you feel a great sense of need? If so, on what level?
   - ❑ problems of life
   - ❑ search for truth
   - ❑ sinful behavior
   - ❑ sinful condition
36. Do you understand the Christian gospel of salvation?
37. Do you sometimes feel helpless and ready to give up?
38. Do you know how to "come to Christ"?
39. Have you ever prayed to be converted?
40. Do you know if anyone is praying for your conversion?
41. Have you ever tried to have a relationship with God?
42. Have you ever come to the point of conversion and then turned away from it?
43. Are you a strong-willed person?
44. Are you aware of any sin that you are unwilling to give up?
45. Are you possibly a backslider?